Lifted

A journey from trauma to triumph

Mike Ritter

Because a sailboat cannot sail directly into the wind to a destination located upwind, a sailor must "tack." The sailor must steer at about a 45-degree angle to the wind direction, tacking, or turning right then left repeatedly at this angle toward the destination.

A "lift" occurs when the wind changes direction such that one can sail at a closer angle to—or even directly to—the desired destination. This reduces the distance and time one must sail to get there.

This concept of being lifted is a metaphor for my life.

My life has been blessed with people, experiences, lessons, and epiphanies that have lifted me to success and fulfillment.

Without them, I would still be "at sea!"

Hence, the title.

Copyrighted Material
Lifted: A journey from trauma to triumph
Copyright © 2019 Mike Ritter
All Rights Reserved.

No part of this publication may be reproduced, stored in a retrieval system or transmitted in any form or by any means—electronic, mechanical, photocopying, recording, or otherwise—without prior written permission from the publisher, except for the inclusion of brief quotations in a review.

For information about this title or to order other books and/or electronic media, contact the publisher:

Atkins & Greenspan Publishing
18530 Mack Avenue, Suite 166
Grosse Pointe Farms, MI 48236
www.twosisterswriting.com

ISBN 978-1-945875-63-2 Hardcover
ISBN 978-1-945875-64-9 Paperback
ISBN 978-1-945875-65-6 eBook

Printed in the United States of America

Cover and Interior design: Van-garde Imagery, Inc.

Contents

	Introduction vii	
Section 1	**Beginnings of a Life Lifted**	
	Chapter 1 Childhood 3	
	Chapter 2 Father Figures 13	
Section 2	**Things That Mattered**	
	Chapter 3 A Young Working Man 29	
	Chapter 4 Friends 35	
Section 3	**Challenges**	
	Chapter 5 Seeking Acceptance 41	
	Chapter 6 I Love Cars! 63	
Section 4	**The Value of Hard Work and Finding Love**	
	Chapter 7 A Strong Work Ethic 75	
	Chapter 8 Shirley: The Greatest Blessing of a Blessed Life! 83	
	Chapter 9 The Trip of a Lifetime and a New Perspective 87	
	Chapter 10 Education 93	
Section 5	**Marriage, Family & Career**	
	Chapter 11 MARRIAGE—Finally!! 103	
	Chapter 12 Wife, Mother, Grandmother 113	
	Chapter 13 An Upward Career Trajectory 119	
	Chapter 14 Finding My Father 127	
	Chapter 15 Enter Christian Science 139	

Section 6	Continental Cablevision & Sailing	
Chapter 16	Moving Back to Michigan	149
Chapter 17	Sailing	157
Chapter 18	City Living—Life in Boston	173
Chapter 19	How and Why Did I Get Here?	181

Afterword 187

Biography: Mike Ritter 191

Introduction

Reflections At 35,000 feet

How I got here!!

> *"The past is a place of reference, not a place of residence, the past is a place of learning, not a place of living."*
>
> —Roy T. Bennett
> *The Light in the Heart:*
> *Inspirational Thoughts for Living Your Best Life*

AN OVERWHELMING SENSE OF awe, gratitude, and clarity suddenly hit me.

How did I get here?

I'm sitting in first class on my way to St. Maarten to join my 66-foot sailboat, crew, and friends to begin a sailing saga that will take me across 15,000 miles of sea to Australia during the next 18 months. A dream come true.

Retired at age 54, with a lakefront home at Lake Tahoe and building a grand home on 40 acres a mile from the ocean near the hamlet of Avila Beach, California, I wonder: *How could one be more blessed?*

One who grew up without a father's presence, with an unstable, promiscuous mother; one who endured horrific challenges, suicide, gangs, and expulsion from high school. One who was forced to attend a trade school, unable to walk for two years as a teenager due to a motorcycle accident, and whose highest goal was to simply get out of school with a job that paid enough for a car and an apartment.

How I got here—and the insights and lessons learned along the way—are the story of my life.

As I look back over the challenges and traumas, what stands out is how every aspect of my life was and continues to be connected in ways that gradually lift and support me on my amazing, blessed journey. I can see how the love and care of so many who touched my life made a huge, positive difference, and how I internalized and applied their wisdom and guidance.

I hope the lessons in my story can make a difference for you.

—Mike Ritter

Section I

Beginnings of a Life Lifted

Chapter 1

Childhood

I HAVE HAD MANY lives. So have most people. We are all changed by circumstance, events, people, and experiences.

Yet many of mine seem so improbable. It's all quite a jumble of memories, feelings, pieces of this and that, of gratitudes, blessings, unwitting mentors, and nightmares. The thought of trying to write about it seemed like straining to make sense of what may make little sense to conventional thought. But, many of those who know a little of my life experience have urged me to write it down: for my children and their children and for those who might gain more insight into their own life experiences.

So, write I have.

And, as I wrote, I found that this is as much for *me* as for my children, grandchildren, and other family members who might have an interest. Although my life offers many lessons, they are mine. We learn from our own experiences, as different as they are. It's folly to think that others can learn vicariously from my lessons. At best, the lessons I share may enlarge your understanding of your experiences. At worst, they will give you a better sense of who I am, or simply be an interesting read.

Nevertheless, I hope that sharing my life story may be useful to help my family to know me better, to better understand their own relationship to me, and maybe even appreciate a bit more about who they are. It is for me because I know this: *all that is really real is now, this moment*. The past is not now; it's not real, much like a dream. Indeed, it is no more real than the future, which has not yet happened.

Yet, my human experiences have had such an impact on me, my values, and motivations. I have found that through my writing, I can embrace a deeper sense of gratitude and wonder at a life truly blessed.

Looking back at the finished product, I am overwhelmed with gratitude. If I had outlined how my life should have been, it could never have come close to how incredible it has been. Through writing these recollections, I so clearly see the single thread that connects all the events in my life, leading to ever higher blessings and goodness—even the good coming from what seemed not so good at the time. I hope you can see this golden thread of goodness in your own life. It is there!!

Early Childhood

According to the record, I was born February 14, 1941, in McMinnville, Oregon. Valentine's Day!

"Oh! So you are a Valentine baby!" So many times I got that kind of reaction when revealing my birth date. As a guy who wanted even the slightest macho image, this just didn't help. But it is a birthday that's easy to remember; a curse when one gets older and would rather forget about it!

My parents were in McMinnville a short time while Mom stayed with her parents. McMinnville is now famous for being home to the huge Spruce Goose, the largest wooden aircraft ever constructed, designed and built by Howard Hughes during World War II.

My mother, Lillian Casey, had married Alexander Stim a year before my birth. When I was born, my father was away in the Navy.

He never left a stateside office during the war. Alex had earned a master's degree in teaching. Mom attended college, but did not finish.

I have very little recollection of my father before my parents separated when I was six. He did not teach as his education had prepared him. He worked for my grandparents, who owned various clothing stores.

Alex Stim and Mike.   Great Grandpa Bell, Mike, Bapo, and Alex.

Given the very strong, domineering personality of my mother's mother, Anna Bell Casey, and her controlling role in my mother's life, it is not surprising that my father tended to be away a lot—and finally left for good. As in virtually everything in my life, his leaving turned out to be very much for the good, as I'll later describe when I located him 30 years later.

Linda, my only full sibling, is two years younger than me. We were fairly close for a time, especially the year following our stepfather Jack Ritter's suicide after we moved to San Francisco.

We later grew up quite apart, even though we were in the same house. Linda had a tough time growing up, taking the brunt of Mom's bitchy and picky nature. She left home for good at age 15. We never shared the mutual support siblings often have for each other as life unfolds. As years and decades passed, we drew further apart to become completely different people with virtually nothing in common except for our parentage.

My Maternal Grandparents

My mother's parents were Albert Berle Casey and Anna B. Bell-Casey. My grandfather went by Berle. I called him Bapo, and I'm told that I named him that before I could say Grandpa. I loved him. He was an oasis in my troubled childhood, but wasn't around much or for very long. I'm told he loved to play cards, stay out late, smoke cigars, and have fun. He was the opposite of my grandmother. She was all business, and very good at it. I remember when my grandmother was asked how many cigars my grandfather had each day; she'd say, "Oh, he smokes two and eats three!"

I called my grandmother Baba. I never really learned the origin of these names, although I understand it means grandmother in an eastern European language. My grandmother was a strong woman who was very controlling. My mother never really disconnected from her dependence on or control of her mother.

My grandmother's parents were Grandpa and Grandma Bell. I never knew their first names. Grandpa Bell was a Methodist minister. He established a church in Ohio and in Washington where I remember visiting them. He was a tall, thin, gentle man. I remember trying to pound nails into pieces of wood in his workshop. He was kind to me. I must have been no more than four years old. I also vaguely remember him baptizing me.

I had originally been baptized Catholic, because my father and his family were very Catholic. When things grew worse between my parents, it was decided that I should be re-baptized Protestant/Methodist. Form over the substance of religion was my family's approach to church.

I can see Grandma Bell in my mind's eye: slim, wrinkled, with a very kind face, and wearing an apron. I'm reminded of them both when I see Grant Wood's *American Gothic* painting of the farmer and wife with a pitchfork: serious, thrifty, and hard-working.

I don't know anything about my grandfather's parents. I'm told they came from Ireland during the potato famine. With the name Casey, it may well be true!

My Maternal Grandparents.

Casey's Redding Store.

My grandparents were business people, especially my grandmother. They owned several clothing stores in succession in Washington, Oregon, and California. The last was in San Francisco's West Portal neighborhood. I remember it because they had it when we (Mom, Lynda, and me) lived in their big, cold house there after Jack Ritter killed himself. My Uncle David, Mom's only sibling, worked in the men's department of his parents' store.

Earlier, when I was about five, we lived in a house that my grandparents owned in San Francisco. The only thing noteworthy about this was that Jerry Brown and his parents lived across the street, and he would bully and beat me up when he could. He was two years older and bigger. His father would become governor of California, as would he, later—indeed, twice!

My Paternal Grandparents

I vaguely remember the one visit to my father's parents. I was no more than four. My grandparents immigrated from Czechoslovakia and lived in the coal mining town of Nesquehoning, Pennsylvania. My grandfather was a coal miner, and neither he nor his wife ever learned English.

They had three sons. My father was the youngest and was by accounts, very spoiled. Yet, this immigrant coal miner put all three sons through college! One son became a priest in the Orthodox Catholic Church, one became a monsignor in the Catholic Church, and one—my father—got a master's degree. Incredible!

The wonder of this heritage has always captivated me. I have somehow always known that this history represents something of who I am; a source of my ethic. My recollection of a single visit when I was not even four years old has stayed with me in vivid detail. I can still see the square, grey, wood-sided houses with sagging front porches. I see the dusty, dirt roads. I remember walking over the railroad track, smelling creosote on railroad ties and getting a Nehi Orange soda with a cousin. I can still taste it. Odd what we remember.

My paternal grandparents.

This captivation is part of what prompted me to find my father 30 years after he left. More on that later.

Fast-forward to a few years ago…

While visiting New York City, I decided to visit Ellis Island to see if I could locate any record of my grandparents. I had tried to do this online a couple years earlier, but couldn't get very far. In the research section at Ellis Island, I located the ship's passenger manifest with my grandfather listed on it. This was an actual copy of the handwritten manifest listing Alex Stim.

Because the steamship companies were responsible for taking anyone back to their point of departure if they were refused admittance to America, the companies did their own screening before departure. Here is the information on the "List or Manifest of Alien Immigrants for the Commissioner of Immigration" for the steamship *Fredric der Grosse* departing Bremen and arriving in New York on October 1, 1902:

Name: Alex Stim

Age: 27

Married

Occupation: Laborer

Able to Read: Yes

Able to Write: Yes

Nationality: Hungary

Last Residence: Hormanne (?)

Seaport for landing in US: Slovak

Final Destination in US: Johnstown, PA

Whether Having a Ticket to Such Destination: Yes

By Whom Was Passage Paid: Friend

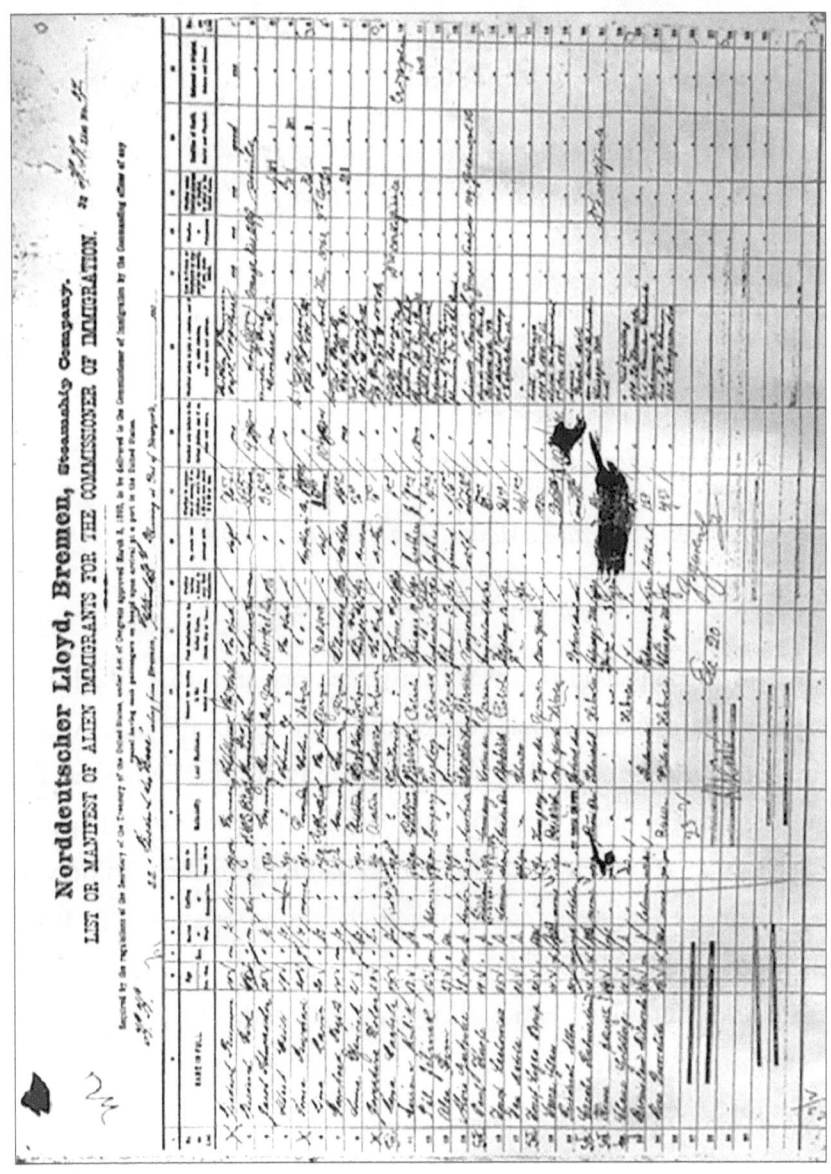

Whether in Possession of Money, if so, whether more than $30 and how much if $30 or less: $16.00

Whether going to join a relative, and if so, what relative, their name and address: Friend of Sgive Gyorgy, Johnstown, PA, 18 Parker Street

Ever in Prison or Almshouse or Supported by Charity: No

Whether a Polygamist: No

Whether under Contract, express or implied to labor in the US: No

Condition of Health, Mental and Physical: Good

Deformed or Crippled, Nature and Cause: No

This made real all that was in my memory and what I had only vaguely heard about. It was very emotional to be in the place where my grandfather passed along with thousands of others who had the great courage to find a better life and endure whatever it took to get it.

We owe so much to these pioneers—our rootstock: mine and our nation's. I sometimes wonder if the years separating us from these courageous immigrants have resulted in a decline in the work ethic and victimless values they brought to the US. It does say something about the ignorance of the anti-immigrant policy gaining support today as I write this.

Chapter 2

Father Figures

Most of my early childhood recollection is of life with my mother and grandmother. I have a vague remembrance of being with both parents, though none being only with my father. I've seen a few home movies showing my father in the picture. I have a dim memory of him in a T-shirt on a hot Sacramento summer day drinking beer in the kitchen when I was maybe three.

My father must have been away in the Navy a lot. I know we—Mom, Lynda, and I—lived for a while in my grandparents' house in San Francisco. I don't remember my father ever being there, but I was only three or four then.

I do recall an image of me sitting alone on the curb in front of the daycare center I attended. I was terrified that my mother had forgotten to pick me up—that she had completely forgotten me—that I was abandoned. I don't know how long I sat there, but it seemed like an eternity.

"Why are you crying?" she asked when she finally arrived. "Why are you so upset?"

"I was scared that I had been forgotten," I told her.

"Do you know how foolish you are to think that? You'd better straighten up!"

What I needed was a big hug, but Mom had to defend herself, unable to see my need.

After San Francisco, we lived in a tract house in Cupertino when my father worked at a women's clothing store in downtown San Jose. I remember lying in bed terrified with my parents yelling and banging. It was incredibly scary, as if my security, my very foundation, had vanished and had been replaced by screaming, threatening demons. My mother has told me that Alex physically abused me by hitting or throwing me. I have no recollection of that. She said he once broke her nose.

An episode I recall was playing with another boy and girl around some new house construction in an open, dug-out basement. I was throwing rocks, trying to get them over the top, when one of the rocks hit the side and fell on the girl's head. She started crying as blood trickled down her face from the cut. She ran home.

I was very frightened and felt I had nowhere to go. I was afraid to go home for fear of being beaten. I must have stayed away for hours before creeping up to our house as it was getting dark. I crept up to the window and heard my parents talking about me. Whatever they said did not comfort me. I don't remember what happened after I ultimately went into the house.

It was while living here that I remember starting school. I can see myself getting on the school bus and feeling lost at what seemed a gigantic school structure. I just don't remember anything good about this time in life.

My parents split up while we were living in Cupertino. My mother would later say he just left us. She would also say that a priest or other counselor advised her to get away from him because of the physical abuse. Whatever the reason, I learned many years later that his leaving was a very good thing.

My next memory is of living in a duplex in San Jose. My dim recollection of this focuses on returning home from school. I was six. All the doors were locked, and Mom was not home. I had to go to the bathroom so very badly. I tried to wait for her, but couldn't make it—I went to the rear of the house and crapped my pants. I felt so humiliated. When my mother finally came home, she castigated me, adding to my deep humiliation.

My father re-entered our lives while we lived in the duplex. I don't know how long he had been away, probably a few months, but he came back just before Christmas. He brought presents for my sister and me. Mine was a Lionel train set. Wow! It was so cool, with a front light on the locomotive. When I put a little pill in the smokestack, it puffed smoke. I loved it, but even then, I had a sense that this gift was to buy some goodwill or simply to show off to Mom.

Not long after, he came with a beautiful new convertible and a very pretty woman to take my sister and me to the boardwalk at Santa Cruz. It was fun, but the whole thing felt strange to me. I remember feeling that if I really enjoyed it, I would be betraying my mother. Mom told us not to call him "Dad," but Alex. I knew that was to hurt him. I don't remember ever calling him Dad anyway. That is the last time I saw my father until 30 years later when I decided it was time to find him and close an unfinished chapter in my life.

What's in a Name? Stim to Ritter

I must have been about seven when we moved from the duplex to a house on Mt. Hamilton View Drive; a long name for a very short street off E. 31st Street in San Jose. My grandmother bought the house for us. Mom met Jack Ritter when we were living here. I don't know how they met, but like most later relationships, it was probably at a bar. Jack had two daughters from a previous marriage. I think his wife had died. Mom and Jack got married, but I don't remember any of that. I do remember Jack and his daughters moving in and filling the house. I also remember my mother's screaming tirades, especially at my older step sister.

This was not a harmonious house. Jack Ritter was a heavy drinker. They would sometimes play cards at the house with neighbors. Jack would get very drunk. When they played at the neighbor's house, Jack would have to be carried home. I don't know how this was done, as Jack was big and tall. Jack managed a brand-new Union Oil gas station. The grand opening included balloons and treats. I recall being told that a customer had crashed into one of the gas pumps on this day, which tended to spoil the grand opening.

Jack's and Mom's relationship was rocky, marked by the ever-present yelling and screaming and stomping about. But Jack was never violent, as far as I know. I was in the second grade and was making a few friends amongst neighbor boys who attended the same school to which we walked. It was here that my Mom decided that I use the last name of Ritter instead of Stim. So, that's what I did. No legal procedures were involved. I just started going by Ritter, and have ever since.

I know very little of Jack Ritter's history, only that he had a sister and family living in Marin County whom we visited after his death and who took his two daughters. The name Ritter means knight in German, though I think Jack was of French, not German extraction.

A Boy's Great Trauma

"Mike, come up here quick," screamed my Mom with terror.

I ran upstairs to her bedroom and found her trying to wrestle Jack to the floor. He had hanged himself from the closet bar. I have a fuzzy recollection that I helped cut him down with a knife that I retrieved from my room, which was next to theirs. I can still see him on the floor. His face is red and blotchy, and spittle is oozing from his mouth. He was dead, despite the bubbly spittle. Mom yelled to one of my half-sisters downstairs to call an ambulance.

"Now, you cannot tell anyone what happened," Mom told me. "Say that he died of a heart attack if anyone asks how he died. You're now the man of the house."

I was eight years old!

The rope Jack used to hang himself was one with a hangman's knot that I had tied in it and left in my room. I was then a Cub Scout and we were learning knots. What kid wouldn't like tying a hangman's knot if he knew how?

Even at the time, I was shocked and just couldn't fathom how this man could have gone into my room, taken my rope that I had tied, and used it to kill himself. It's inconceivable that a grown man with a wife who was then pregnant—with two children of her own and two by his previous marriage and no source of income aside from his—would kill himself. And, to do it in his own house for his family to witness and deal with, using the knot his stepson tied! To be that sick and able to function in any way in everyday life is impossible to understand. I still wonder how a man of six feet could possibly hang himself to death from a closet bar that isn't over five feet high. He could have been very drunk. Maybe he and my mom were playing some weird, sick games.

On this evening that was dark in every way, the ambulance arrived with sirens and lights. Jack's body was wheeled out of the house on a gurney as lots of neighbors congregated.

I understand that Jack had taken out a life insurance policy a few months earlier, but it did not pay out because suicide was excluded. What a dumb guy, if this were part of his death plan. It would be comical, if not so tragic.

A mystery to me. I tried learning more about this touchy subject from Mom over the years, but she would just go spacey and say, "I don't remember," when asked for anything that would help me understand what really happened.

Cold San Francisco

I don't remember the events of the following few days. I do know that Jack's two daughters went to live with his sister in Marin County. Mom, Lynda, and I went to San Francisco to live with my grandmother and grandfather (Baba and Bapo) in their big, impressive house. My memory of it all was grey, cold emptiness. I missed my friends and third grade teacher, Miss Moreno. She read stories to the class. One of them was from a book that I brought—one of the several *Wizard of Oz* books I loved.

I started the fourth grade in San Francisco. I had a very difficult time—scholastically and emotionally. I hated school; my memories of it are cold, colorless, and friendless.

My grandfather, whom I loved, was not around much. It was during this time that my grandparents split up and divorced, leaving me feeling even more lonely. His absence was a blow that I didn't need.

My Uncle David, Mom's brother, cared about me. I liked being with him. He lived in SF with his wife, Norma, and their baby daughter, Faye. He worked in my grandparents' clothing store, as did my mom. He had been a Navy fighter pilot, flying from aircraft carriers in World War II. He was shot down and suffered some injuries, which later caused his death.

After leaving San Francisco, Uncle David moved with his family to Portland, Oregon, and lived in a house next to his wife's parents. I remember visiting them at age 14 or 15. I enjoyed being with him and recall joining him on a business road trip where he called on businesses as a salesman for S&H Green Stamps. It was fun. He died a few years later from brain cancer that was attributed to his war injuries. He was a good person who was finally able to get away from his domineering mother, though I think that difficult environment took its toll on him, as it did my mother.

Uncle David

While in San Francisco, Mom gave birth to my half-sister, Kathy, whose father was Jack Ritter. Mom had a nanny care for Kathy and watch Lynda and me. This enabled her to work at my grandmother's clothing store a few blocks away. Mom was dating a couple of men then. I remember going with them to the Sutro Baths to swim. These baths were very famous and old. Built in 1886, this was a massive, glass-enclosed spa resembling the baths of imperial Rome. Six saltwater swimming pools were heated to different temperatures. Some had very high, steep water slides that were great fun because you could really get going fast on the way down and surf off the end. Sutro Baths were destroyed by fire in 1966.

A Summer Oasis

It was a very cold, bleak, and lonely summer at my Grandmother's house in San Francisco where we moved after stepfather Jack Ritter killed himself. I was without my friends. The city that can be grey and cold in the summer was matched by the mood of my mother who was very pregnant with Jack's baby and didn't handle stress well in the best of times.

My grandparents had divorced earlier that year. This compounded my loneliness because I really loved my grandfather and felt close to him. Although I had not spent a lot of time with him, when I did, it fed me. I just knew he loved me. I've learned that it isn't how much time you spend with another that enriches, but the attention and love expressed. It felt good to be with him. But he was gone. He was living with a woman and her young daughter on the Colville Indian Reservation in eastern Washington near Grand Coulee Dam. He worked for his brother, who managed the general store in this very small town of Nespelem.

It was arranged that I would spend a month with him that summer of 1949 when I was eight. It would be a real adventure! Eager to leave that dark environment, I felt no hesitation or fear. I remember boarding a DC3 twin engine, propeller-driven airplane. The stewardess was great at "mothering" me on the trip. I don't remember how many landings and take-offs we made on the way, but they were the best part of the trip, aside from the unbelievable views from just 5,000 feet. I loved the vibration, noise, acceleration, then lift off. What eight-year-old wouldn't love that!

My grandfather met me at the airport. I remember the impressive sight of Grand Coulee Dam as we drove by. He lived in a very small house. I shared a bedroom with his woman friend's daughter, who was probably five years older than me. I didn't think they liked my intruding on them as a grandson from a previous marriage, but that had little effect on my joy that summer.

The town was really small. Its current population is 235, which was probably the same back then. In the general store, where my grandfather worked, a thick layer of sawdust covered the floors. It smelled like the insides of a cedar chest. It was fun to see all the stuff for sale, from hardware and plumbing to bags of rice and corn. A watermelon cost 2-1/2 cents a pound. So, an eight-pound watermelon cost 20 cents! The town also had a small movie theater with benches for seating. I remember watching the movie *Nature Boy* there along with a newsreel presenting the latest news. The newsreel showed a fighter jet blowing up a barn with its rockets—the latest in aerial warfare.

I ran around all day with several local Native American kids who were about my age. This was a precursor to the later friendships I would have with several Mexican guys and their families. The best part was learning to swim and play in a sawmill pond.

This pond was half full of logs floating and waiting to be milled. We would have contests rolling the logs under our feet to see how long and how fast we could spin the log without falling in the water. Think about climbing upon a wobbly log, then balancing well enough to get it spinning and not fall off!! I definitely fell off amid many laughs, and learned to dog paddle as a necessity! I think this was as close to a Huckleberry Finn summer as one can get. I completely forgot about the life I left behind and thought little about having to return to it soon.

Other wonderful recollections of that summer include the amazing moccasins that I got. They were the real thing! I still remember their smoky smell, wonderfully soft feel, and beautiful beading. I wish I still had them. When I held or wore them, I felt warm and happy.

One early morning before dawn, my grandfather and I went out to dig worms for fishing. After collecting a bunch, we drove to a remote spot near a noisy stream where my grandfather taught me how to rig and bait the hook and cast it up stream. We caught several pan-sized trout within an hour or so and had a wonderful lunch back home. No, it was the best lunch I had ever tasted!!

That summer oasis had finally come to an end when my grandfather drove me all the way back to cold San Francisco. Boy, I remember how depressing that felt. Instead of comforting me, my grandmother's only interest seemed to be to learn what my grandfather and his lady friend were about and whether he or she "pumped" me for information about her. This all seemed very confusing and heartless to a lonely eight-year-old.

School would be starting soon at a new school, in the fourth grade with no friends. But I would always remember that amazing summer—an oasis to visit in my mind whenever I wanted or needed it. I've since learned that such experiences are the unfolding good in our lives that help heal and overcome challenges. Remembering these—and the warm feelings they bring—can lift us whenever needed. They are always there for us.

The Revolving Bedroom Door

I don't remember the circumstances of moving back to our house in San Jose, but given that my grandmother still owned it and we had spent a couple of years there previously, returning was natural. This familiar place with the friends I knew, attending the same school again, felt good. I was then in the fifth grade. My favorite teacher, Miss Moreno, seemed happy to see me back, but she showed no spark of connection that I thought we had back in third grade. Nevertheless, she played an important, comforting role at a very critical time.

Mom continued dating. She would meet men in bars. One night she came home crying and telling me that she was bawled out by others at a bar for pursuing men so soon after her husband, Jack Ritter, had died. She was looking for my sympathy and support! But there were always men who would spend the night with her. I recall one man who was very nice, and he drove a new Chrysler convertible. I thought he was rich and hoped he wouldn't move on as the others always had. I remember Mom proudly showing me the money he'd leave on her dresser and telling me how kind he was, as though I were oblivious to what she was doing. Where was her head?

I know that the butcher at the neighborhood market was also a visitor to Mom's bedroom. I often went to this local market to get milk or bread, but always felt uncomfortable seeing him at the market, knowing he was Mom's "friend." The whole thing felt very wrong and unmentionable. Looking back, I can better understand why several of my friends were not allowed to come to my house. If I wanted to play with them, I had to go to their house or be outside in the neighborhood. Mom's trashy reputation seemed well-known and, sadly, limited my friendships.

One particularly unhappy event involved a bartender Mom was dating. I met him when he came to take her out. Then one day Mom asked me if I would like to go deer hunting with him. That sounded pretty neat. I had thought hunting and shooting a gun would be fun. It also meant I would go somewhere with a man who might care about being with me.

Boy, was I wrong about both. He was supposed to pick me up at a particular time in the morning. Ready to go, I waited by the front door. I waited and waited—let down by another man. I think Mom finally called him to forcefully remind him about it. He finally showed up two hours late. He didn't seem so happy to be taking me.

He had a Hudson car, like an upside-down bathtub. We drove up toward Mt. Hamilton on a very twisty road. I was getting car sick, which seemed to irritate him. He claimed to be looking for a good place to stop to hunt deer. We never found any, but he did offer to stop so I could shoot his rifle a couple times. So, we stopped, and I shot the gun twice. I was surprised at how loud it was and the amount of kick it had. It was not fun after all!

As we drove home, I suggested that we tell everyone that we didn't get a deer, but we saw one and I shot at it and missed. He thought that was a good idea, so that was my story. He soon found a bar and left me to wait in the car while he went inside for a while.

I was happy to finally get home.

A Second Suicide??

Mom started dating Leonard Mendoza regularly and they married within a few months. He worked at San Jose Steel, just across Highway 101. He loved his car: a new 1954 Mercury hardtop. At first, he seemed like a nice enough man, though he did not say much. They didn't get along well from the start. I remember this scene regularly: Mom yelling, followed by long, strained silences, and Leonard pouting, then driving off in a huff.

On at least one occasion when a more serious spat occurred, Leonard gathered a couple bottles of iodine, which were labeled with skull and crossbones indicating that they were poisonous, and loudly threatened to commit suicide by drinking them. I don't think he ever drank any. Even if he had, I think he'd just get sick at worst.

Another time he went to the garage, closed the door and started his car and let it run. He was trying to die by asphyxiation. It didn't work. At least I know that no ambulances came, and I saw him in apparent good health soon after that.

Having witnessed a previous stepfather succeed at doing what Leonard was threatening, it felt like a sick joke to live with someone so deranged or plain mean as to threaten to kill himself.

I find it amazing the amount of trauma a boy (or girl) can survive when given no choice. And survival is often what one learns from a challenging childhood.

These survival skills serve one well in later life, especially when one also learns that there are no victims; that lesson took me longer to learn.

To my knowledge, Mom never drew the line on Leonard's behavior. He stayed with us until I was busted up and in the hospital from the motorcycle accident.

Leonard decided he did not want to deal with an invalid stepson, and he left. Although they got a divorce, Mom claims that it was an annulment, so as to kid herself into believing the marriage never happened.

Section 2

Things That Mattered

Chapter 3

A Young Working Man

Paper Route

Mom dated a circulation manager for *The San Jose Mercury News*. She urged him to give me a paper route. Weird how I can remember his name: Burt Countryman!

At 12 years old, I was one of their youngest paperboys. Although he was reluctant to take me on so young, he agreed to do so probably to keep favor with Mom. It turned out to be a task I responsibly performed for three years! I learned so much.

A paper route is a lot of work. The paper had to be delivered everyday no matter what else I wanted to do that day, or how bad I might be feeling, or how lousy the weather.

Every day after school, I would ride my bike to where the bundles of papers were delivered. My route included about 120 homes in an adjacent neighborhood. First, I had to fold each paper and put a rubber band around it. If the paper had just a few pages that day, say 25 or less, I could box them. Boxing was folding in half lengthwise, then folding in thirds, tucking one end under the other. Other paperboys and I would race each other for who was the fastest boxer. I liked it when the papers could be boxed, because I didn't have to use rubber bands, which I paid for. Besides, throwing boxed papers from my bike as I rode by each house was easier and more accurate than those with a rubber band. When it rained, I had to slip them into plastic bags to keep the papers dry.

On Sunday mornings, the paper was always big and heavy. Having a paper route was very physical: 120 papers are weighty and bulky. I often had to load and carry front and back bags over my shoulders and saddle bags over a rack on the back of my bike.

Once loaded with papers, I had to pedal my bike and maneuver within accurate throwing distance of each house.

In addition to the required perseverance and physical strength, a paper route requires a sense of business, accounting, and finance.

I essentially ran a small business starting at age 12. I had to pay for the papers I delivered. If I got more papers than I had customers, I had to eat the extra cost. So, keeping good subscriber records was essential, and I had to memorize which houses received the paper. Changes were always occurring as people started or stopped their subscriptions.

I was responsible for selling more subscriptions and trying to get each new resident in my territory to subscribe. The more subscribers I had, the more money I could make, since the subscription fee I charged was more than I paid for each paper.

I also had to personally collect that monthly subscription fee from each of my 120 customers every month. That took a lot of time. Often people were not home, or if they were, they would ask me to return when they had the money. Of course, I had to keep track of who hadn't paid. When repeated collection attempts failed, I would stop delivering, but I still had to eat the cost of the papers I delivered to the deadbeats.

When my grandmother learned of the several non-payers on my route, she came with me to collect. She was really brutal with the deadbeats. They deserved it. I learned that you can be nice with people, but had to draw a line beyond which you really needed to be tough. Although it was embarrassing to have her with me, I learned a lot. Besides, it felt good to have her really stick up for me!

Sometimes on cold, rainy Sunday mornings when I started my route at 6:00 a.m., my grandmother would take me around in her car. Accurately throwing papers through the open, passenger-side window wasn't easy, but I kept dry!

I experienced just one attempt to rob me. But the guy failed because he was on foot and I was on my bike; I left him in the dust!

I think I saved as much as $400 from my paper route, plus having spending money—a fair sum 65 years ago!

I do not underestimate the knowledge, values, and discipline that this paper route gave me. Nothing about this kind of training is theoretical. It's really too bad that young people aren't widely offered this kind of opportunity today.

When I think of my three-year paper route and another job I had picking fruit in the summers to earn money—getting up before light, riding my bike to the orchards, and working until exhausted for 10 cents per bucket of prunes—I'm grateful for the important lessons learned: lessons about commitment, persistence, hard work, economics, bookkeeping, reliability, saving, and so on.

Young people today have very few such opportunities. There are no orchards nearby anymore. When is the last time you saw a paperboy? Child labor laws today would probably prevent such employment anyway. A bit of over protection.

Accordion Lessons (*not so fondly remembered*)

I must have been eight years old or so when Mom decided I should take accordion lessons. We rented one at first, and later she bought my very own accordion. An accordion is big, bulky, heavy (especially for growing kids), and they can pinch! You have to keep pulling and pushing the left side, and you can't see the buttons you have to play with your left hand.

Playing the accordion tended to be torturous. I never liked it, but I practiced because of my mother's endless screaming threats if I didn't. I must have taken lessons for up to two years, which is hard to believe.

San Jose used to hold the title of having the most parades of any town its size in the US. The accordion store where I took lessons would participate in some of them. I still have this comical vision of me sitting with a bunch of other kids harnessed to our accordions—sitting on the back of a large flatbed truck crawling along the parade route—as we're trying to play a tune together!

That memory reminds me of the comedy where an awkward kid plays a cello in a marching band and has to constantly move his chair forward to catch up with the band, play quickly, then move it again.

The traumatic exposure to this instrument turned me off to any future with music. However, as I'll describe later, I quickly connected deeply with jazz—especially piano jazz while recovering from the motorcycle accident.

Not until I was 65 years old, did I finally get over the resistance to music lessons, and started taking jazz piano lessons, which feeds my soul.

Those accordion lessons had a lasting effect on me. I can humorously laugh and share the experience—and it turns out others are like me. I was recently in a piano store in Reno looking at upright pianos. After finding one that would do, a conversation with the store owner led him to share how he would get nauseated whenever he even saw a musical symbol. He attributed it to a traumatic experience as a child forced to play an instrument.

That instrument? An accordion!

I shared my story and we both laughed hysterically.

Then he told me this story:

"A man owned and professionally played a very valuable accordion. He was on a road trip and had the instrument in the back of his station wagon. Needing a break, he went into a bar for a drink, and while sitting at the bar, he worried that he might have left his car unlocked with his valuable accordion in the back. So, he quickly rushed out to his station wagon and was relieved to find that he had indeed locked it. Then he was shocked to see that someone had broken out the rear window! He was puzzled to see that his accordion was still where he left it, but… next to it was another accordion!!"

This scene still makes me laugh. I guess something is universally humorous about the accordion, at least for those no longer traumatized by being forced to play one.

I'm so glad I am now one of those!

My Mexican Connection: Picking Fruit

For a few weeks during the summer when I was 10 and 11 years old, I rode my bike with a friend to the prune orchards about two miles away from our house to start picking fruit by 7:00 a.m. We were very much the minority, as the other pickers were Mexican families: babies, kids, even grandparents. They generally did not speak English.

My goal was to earn money for the extra things I wanted: a BB gun, a better bike, model airplanes, some clothes.

What I really got from that job were the seeds of appreciation for the expression of family, love, and caring, as well as the happy chatter and laughter of Mexicans together "at work." And work they did.

Mexicans "at work" never seemed burdened. And, no matter how hard I tried to quickly fill my bucket with the prunes I picked, I could never match their effortless speed. This appreciation grew greatly over the next few years and, I think, helped to form some of my values.

I worked hard to fill my bucket with prunes, getting my card punch for each full bucket I produced. At the end of the day, around 5:00 p.m., I would turn my card in and get paid, maybe $2 or $3.

Boy, I was so pooped at the end of the day that the bike ride home was work. But I think I felt a sense of achievement, of worthiness.

I also cut apricots. I cut them in half, discarding the pit and placing them on large drying trays. I got paid by the trays I filled. Again, the Mexicans were so fast, I was embarrassed. But it was money!!

I also made an attempt to pick string beans. Oh my, the constant stooping was excruciating. I only lasted one day! But the Mexicans did this day after day without complaint.

This was my first introduction to hard work, as well as to people who had an incredible work ethic and values that helped lift me and refine my priorities as I later made Mexican friends.

Chapter 4

Friends

While in junior high school, I was drawn to friendship with several Mexican fellows. I remember playing with one friend in the acres of empty fruit crates in an industrial yard. These thousands of wooden crates were about 2' by 2' by 3' long and were stacked 15 feet high. We would move them around and make magical passages, tunnels, and secret rooms, very much like an underground maze. We never got caught, or we would have surely gotten into big trouble, but it was great fun. It fired our imaginations. I think Tom Sawyer and Huck Finn would have loved it!!

This friend invited me to his house. He had several brothers and sisters who, when I came, would yell enthusiastically, "It's Mike Reeeter! It's Mike Reeeter!"

His parents always invited me to stay for dinner if it was late afternoon. I was treated as one of the family—enveloped in the warmth of happy chatter, the different but comforting food, and his parents' calmness and support.

I suppose my memory is a bit rose-colored here, but it surely was like getting a cool drink in a parched desert compared to the atmosphere at my house.

Another friend had an uncle who owned a tortilla factory and Mexican bakery. Several weekend mornings, we both went to help.

The cornmeal for tortillas would go into a hopper and the machine would measure it out, roll it into flat rounds, and convey it on a belt through the oven. The tortillas would emerge as hot balls that flattened as they cooled, moving down the belt toward me. I would count a dozen, place them in a plastic bag, and seal the end. I think one of the most delicious things ever are hot tortillas—just out of the oven, rolled up with butter—*muy, muy rico!!*

This friend later moved to Los Angeles. I missed him. I had his address, so when I ran away from home at age 15, after hitchhiking from San Jose to southern California, I went to his house in LA in the middle of the night. I was really disappointed that he did not seem so pleased to see me—nor were his parents. As I think about the circumstances, what did I expect?

Getting Help for a Friend

I used to ride my bike to Alum Rock Park and up a trail beside a creek to fish. It was probably a five- to six-mile ride each way from home. I usually caught a couple of small trout and was as thrilled about that as the beauty and quiet of what felt like a very remote oasis.

One day I rode my bike there with two friends: Don Leonetti and Stan Blanchard. We rode far up the trail beside the creek. On the way down, Don careened off the trail and crashed. He was badly hurt and couldn't get up. Stan and I were panicked and knew we needed help. We were far from the park proper and no one was around. Stan said he'd stay with Don and for me to get help. I was really scared and did not want to take this on, but knew that I simply must. Don needed help. I rode as fast as possible without wiping out. Back at the park, I found a maintenance man who directed me to an office where they called an ambulance. I waited so I could direct them to Don. They carried him down on a stretcher and off to a hospital.

I rode home and later called his parents, who told me he had a badly broken leg. I visited him in the hospital and many times at his home. A huge cast covered his body. We played lots of cards and watched wrestling on TV. I enjoyed our visits while simply being with a friend. We continued to do a few things together after he was back on his feet, but our friendship did not endure because, I think, he later moved away.

A Black Family's Warmth

George Washington was the only black kid in my grammar school. Although we were friendly, we were not "friends." I was well aware of his color and I saw how some kids shunned him because of it.

I delivered papers to his house—an old, weathered, wooden house with a sagging front porch. Many times when I was making my collection rounds, George's dad would invite me in for juice or hot cocoa. I well remember the warmth and kindness his parents showed me. Their house was very clean and neat and had a feeling of grounded calmness. George's Dad took the time to talk with me about how I was doing, and asked about my paper route and my aspirations. He was such a kind, caring man. Getting to know this wonderful family, I became conscious of how wrong it was to judge George by his color. This black family certainly saw me without prejudice. Yet, I knew prejudice and unfair judgment, as it was directed at me from kids of white families who knew of my "loose" mother and lack of father at home.

I am so very grateful for so many of these "Things that Mattered." They elevated my thoughts about family, unconditional love, hard work, joy, and laughter. I had very little exposure to these qualities in my dysfunctional family. Nevertheless, they were supplied to me in unanticipated ways. And they were shaping the foundation of who I am.

SECTION 3

Challenges

Chapter 5

Seeking Acceptance

"I Have No Father"

It seems like people often asked, "Where is your father?"

"I don't have a father," I always responded.

Of course, the reply to that was generally, "Everyone has a father."

It's strange, but I never had an answer that was satisfactory to me. I could have simply said, "My parents got a divorce," which was true. I think that the varied circumstances around the many men that paraded through my life left me so confused or perplexed that I couldn't sort it out enough to answer that simple question.

I know that this confusion left me troubled. I remember when I was hanging out with three friends one night in the alley behind the store owned by my friend's father. One of the guys, Bob Schiro, began taunting me and making fun of me for having "no father." I asked him to stop, but he continued. I got so mad that I just slugged him hard in the face. Wow, the response was immediate silence and contrition. He never bothered me again. I felt so strong and proud and that a big weight had lifted from me. I gained immediate respect from my friends who were there. No doubt the frustration from the difficulty in handling the "no father" dilemma had lifted that night.

Gangs

The East Side of San Jose had gangs. They were not like the large drug-funded, armed criminal gangs of today. There were the white gangs and Mexican gangs. My gang was the "Blood Brothers." The major rival Mexican gang was the "Blue Velvets." They had really cool velvet jackets. Ours were just okay.

We had occasional "rumbles," or gang fights. I was only in one, and it turned out to be pretty much a stand off. But, if I were bothered at the local dance/recreation center, I would rely on other Blood Brothers coming to my aid. These fights did not involve guns then; mostly fists, feet, and knives. One of my friends was stabbed to death in one of these gang fights. But, compared to the gang situation of today, this was pretty tame.

Nevertheless, I never reconciled how I could fight to injure another who had done nothing to me. I would regularly skip school with other gang members. One of them had a car, so we would just cruise around. Sometimes we'd go as far as "Playland" at the beach in San Francisco.

It's strange to think that I belonged to a white gang that fought Mexican gangs when I had a deepening affection for Mexicans from my personal experiences. I'm not sure I can reconcile it, except that the majority of my friends were white and their gang had to be mine. Sadly, I was really just a follower then. But, I needed to belong, even if I knew it really didn't fit my then-shallow sense of who I was.

Dangerous Adventures

The Brick Factory Caper. Stan Blanchard, Gary Garretson, and I were close friends who were always looking for excitement in the neighborhood. One Saturday, we ventured across Highway 101 just two blocks away, when it had a stoplight at Santa Clara Street. We were riding our bikes and decided to leave them and jump the fence at the big brick factory, which was closed that day. Amidst countless pallets of bricks and cement blocks around the yard, a lift truck was calling our name! We found that the key was in it and we could start it. At 13 years old, we each itched to drive something—anything. This was it. We took turns, wildly driving around the yard, "accidentally" knocking over several of the stacked blocks.

We were having a great time when someone drove to the gate and opened it to drive in. We panicked, dove for the fence, and ran. Then we realized that we had left our bikes behind. By the time we got the courage to attempt to retrieve them, the police had arrived and corralled them. What to do? Turn ourselves in, or abandon our most important possessions?

We decided to turn ourselves in. The police took down lots of information from us and the brick company employee. We were terrified that we would be taken to jail when we were ushered into the police car. The policeman said they really should take us to jail, but if we would never do this sort of thing again, they said they would take us home and talk to our parents. Neither was a great option, but jail was way worse. As we drove to our homes, two of us who were attending a week-long summer camp the following week, feared that we would be unable to go as punishment. After a long screaming lecture, I was able to attend camp, as was my friend. So, we had our bikes, summer camp, and a scary adventure that turned out ok.

A Policeman in My Bedroom. My prized possession was a .22 rifle that I bought on mail order. Yes, a 13-year-old could buy a real gun then. I would have target practice in the backyard and enjoyed cleaning and oiling it. One day I decided to take a few shots out the back window of my second story bedroom! I don't remember what the heck I was shooting at when a giant of a policeman came into my room saying, "What the hell are you doing?" The shock of it nearly loosened my bowels! Turns out, a neighbor saw what I was doing and called the police. No one was home, so the cop came right up to my room.

Well, that time I *was* taken to the police station downtown. That was a frightening ride. After some paperwork and a lecture, I was told that they would keep my gun until my parents came to get it. Then they called my Mom, who came to get me. Somehow I got the gun back sometime later. I still have it. We use it occasionally to try to control our pesky rabbit problem on the farm. I'm not proud of this very stupid behavior. I could have really hurt someone. I was fortunate. Another lesson learned the hard way.

An Attempted Get-Away

Life continued to be awful at home. My mother was in her worst form in the mornings. She would scream, yell, and pick about the smallest things. I couldn't wait to get out of the house and head for school or to my friends' house to walk to school with them.

My friend Stuart lived a few houses away. I always went to his house to meet him so we could walk to junior high school together. His dad made him polish his shoes every morning, even if he was running late. Stuart and I made and flew model airplanes together. I really enjoyed that. We also had great fun reading *Mad Magazine* and memorizing some of the silly stuff like: "It takes a heap of homing to make a pigeon toed." I know his parents did not approve of his being friends with me—nothing verbal, they were just very cold toward me. He was never allowed to come to my house. That was just as well, because I didn't want friends over.

Another friend was Danny Waldrop. He was a year or so older than me. We began plotting a scheme to take off and go to San Diego, where we would get jobs working on fishing boats. I was 15. I had money saved from my paper route—about $300, which was a large amount then. So, one day when no one was home, I wrote a "goodbye, don't worry" note to Mom and left it under my sister's pillow to be found later.

Then we were off. Each carrying a suitcase, we started hitchhiking on Highway 101 toward Los Angeles. We would tell those who gave us a lift that we were joining the Navy in San Diego. Just a few rides got us all the way to LA.

We were dropped at a gas station where we asked two guys for a ride. They agreed, but required that we first fill their gas tank. We did that, and before we could get in, they drove off laughing! At least they left our suitcases beside the gas pumps. Somehow we got to LA, where we looked up my Mexican friend whom I described earlier. We had hoped to spend the night at his house, but that didn't work out. We found some flop house for the night. I remember being propositioned by some nasty old man. That scared me.

I think we took the bus to San Diego. We found a cheap room and met a couple guys who would show us around and buy liquor for us. I bought a switchblade knife that gave me some comfort, but deep down, I wasn't so sure. At the same time, I was intent on getting a tattoo. But, because I couldn't prove I was over 18, I needed to provide written consent from my parents. So I wrote a note of approval and forged my Mom's signature. Fortunately, the ploy didn't work, so I never got that cool tattoo.

We spent one day and night in Tijuana, Mexico. Then it was a very down-and-out, raucous place—nothing but bars and slums. We drank a lot, got sick, and returned to San Diego. I must say that I never felt comfortable doing any of the things we did since leaving San Jose. None of it felt right. But, staying home was not a good option for me, either.

One morning before dawn, we went to the fishing boat docks looking for that job. The couple of fishing boat guys we asked just shrugged us off. As we walked, we were approached by two policemen. They asked us who we were and what we were doing. My mother had alerted the police of my disappearance and an "All Points Bulletin" or "APB" was sent out for authorities to watch for us. The police identified us as the missing truants and took us in. We were able to get our things from the "hotel," although they confiscated my way-cool switchblade knife.

We were ultimately taken to a juvenile detention facility, or "Juvenile Hall." We were issued drab coveralls to wear and assigned a bunk. I stayed two days and nights. Despite the sinister-looking inmates, with danger indicated by the fact that we could only eat with plastic spoons, I was not frightened.

I was secretly relieved that this "adventure" of about nine days was over. My mother drove from San Jose to pick me up. She was uncharacteristically quiet and subdued. She told me how much I had hurt her, but thankfully she did not yell or scream. She never asked why I ran away! And I never saw Danny Waldrop again.

The Non-Student

I never connected with school. I was so distracted by trying to be a part of the "drop-out" element, I simply put no effort into school. As my focus was elsewhere, I fell behind, causing me to dislike school even more. I was often late to school with no acceptable explanation—despite my failed attempts to write an excuse note and sign my mother's name. I usually went to my friend Gary Garretson's house and rode with him in his almost-new, really cool, yellow Ford convertible. We often arrived late to school.

I did not participate in any extracurricular activities. In my circle, they were considered for sissies. Nor did I ever play sports. I didn't think I would be any good at it anyway, based on my poor performance on the playground in grammar school. I think I was usually the last person picked for a team! I missed a great deal by not playing sports, but it just never even entered my thoughts as anything I'd want to do. Plus, I received absolutely no encouragement to do so at home. In truth, this was part of my deepening sense of isolation. As a result, my attendance, grades, and behavior went from bad to worse.

On several occasions, my "parents" (meaning my Mother) and I were summoned by the school principal to discuss my poor behavior. My grandmother attended a couple of these as well. It was always embarrassing. During the last visit, the principal suggested, or rather insisted that it would be better if I attended San Jose Technical High School where I could learn a trade—something that would at least enable me to get a job. College was not considered even a remote possibility. Since the school was required to keep me in classes until I graduated or turned 18, moving me to a school with lots of "shop" classes made sense for a very low-potential student.

So, off I went to San Jose Tech High. I chose aircraft mechanics.

Besides four hours of shop each day, I took three required subjects: history, math, and English. Most of the students were there for the same reason: they weren't making it in an academic environment. And, the teachers were not the best of the lot. Mine was an alcoholic whose attendance record was as bad as mine!

I learned nothing in the academic subjects, but I did learn to play dice and toss coins for money. I also learned a few things about mechanics from working on an old World War II radial aircraft engine. We also worked on Continental engines still in use today. That helped me later when I had a job as an auto mechanic and worked on my own hot rod cars.

Tech High was on the other side of town. I had a small, one cylinder motorcycle that I rode to school. I loved to ride it. The sense of freedom was wonderful. Of course, those were the days before helmets were required. Besides, at 15, I was invincible—or so I thought.

A Life-Changing Event

"WHAM!" A loud thud in blackness. Next I knew, I was laying on the ground with several people standing around me. I tried to get up, feeling only terrible pain and a sickening, weird, crunchy feeling in my legs that would not move. An ambulance arrived.

Just before this, I was riding on the back of my friend's motorcycle. My motorcycle was at his house, where we were repairing the motor I had fried by running it out of oil. We were traveling down an undivided, four-lane road at about 60 miles per hour when a pickup truck coming the opposite way made a left turn over double white lines in front of us, as the truck entered an orchard on our right.

We laid the bike down—which means making a hard turn to make the bike lay on its side, close to the ground. The goal is to either slide off or slide under the vehicle, or at least avert a head-on collision.

My friend was able to slide off. I stayed on the bike and struck the truck at its rear fender. Both femurs (thigh bones) snapped completely in two. Incredibly, it turned out that I had no other serious injuries despite enduring a force strong enough to break the two biggest bones in the body!

After a painful ambulance ride (I still remember crossing those bumpy railroad tracks by the cannery), I don't recall anything until after the surgeries when I awoke in bed with my legs strung up in traction. Cables, pulleys, and weights were all over. I had lost a lot of blood in my legs, which had caused some concern about my survival. I took over eight pints of blood.

When it was clear that I would live, the doctor told my mother that I may never walk again. A rod inserted into the marrow of my right leg was keeping the bones together. A plate was screwed over the break in my left leg. I spent one month in the hospital on this first of several hospital stays. Over the next 18 months, all of the hardware was removed. Fortunately, I didn't know then that this saga would consume two years of my life.

Before leaving the hospital for the first time, a cast extended from my armpit down my right leg, around my chest and waist, and down to my ankle. I wore this cast for eight or nine months. After a few months, I could move from bed to walker, but could not stand long, nor could I bend at the waist to sit. The body cast kept me board-straight. So, I'd soon get back in bed, whose overhead bar enabled me to move myself a bit.

I won't detail all of the medical stuff that occurred over the next two years. More important are those events that had such meaning for me during this difficult time.

We Move. While I was first in the hospital, stepfather #3—Leonard Mendoza—told Mom that he did not want to deal with an invalid boy. So, he left. At least he was out of my life, after having messed with it for the prior six months. When I finally left the hospital, I was taken by ambulance to our new house. We had moved from our house off East 31st Street, where I lived since age six, except for that cold year in San Francisco, to the suburb of Willow Glen. Again, my grandmother bought the house.

Bedridden Mike, Kathy, and Darrel.

Willow Glen was a more upscale area—and very white compared to East San Jose! Although I never really connected with the area, I did finally graduate from high school here. Plus, this is where

I lived when I met Shirley. My best friend here was Jim Huntsinger. We sure had a lot of fun messing with cars and cruising around.

This move was especially meaningful because it completed a total break from my messy past. I had no friends carry over from East San Jose. In fact, I don't remember any of them visiting me in the hospital. Not only had the pattern of my life changed completely by being bedridden, it was taking place in a totally new external environment. I think this total newness had a subtle, but real, impact on my new beginnings.

Home Teachers. One of the most important influences on my growth and values was the blessing of a "home teacher" that the school provided for shut-ins. Because I was unable to attend school for nearly two years, a teacher came to me at home, one hour per day. The two different teachers were so kind and caring. The most wonderful part was that they devoted their entire focus for a whole hour on just me.

Learning became exciting! My reading improved and I enjoyed learning new things. In the beginning, I did my homework to please them. Then I did it because it became a fun, mental adventure that I enjoyed while just laying in bed. I remember reading *Uncle Tom's Cabin* by Harriet Beecher Stowe and discussing it with the teacher. What a revelation to discover that so much meaning was packed into what seemed like a simple story.

These two wonderful teachers inspired me to value learning and the discipline associated with it. I have such gratitude for that opportunity, a major aspect of the divine unfolding that began at my birth and continues to this day. I hope the thread of this unfolding—these non-random blessings—is apparent as you read this. This is the true miracle of my life. I hope you can see them in your life, too.

Crochet Therapy. My grandmother had always knitted. So, when she finally stopped owning and managing clothing stores, she eventually became a yarn manufacturer's representative; she sold yarn at wholesale to yarn stores. And, she was very good at it. She sold to knitting shops in Washington, Oregon, and California. I remember one sales trip when she took me with her. She would introduce me as her son, telling me that if her clients knew I was her grandson, they would figure out how old she was. I didn't get the point. It just seemed silly and vain to me.

Her age had nothing to do with the quality of her yarn or value of her service. More troubling was simply the dishonesty of it—and if here, where else? She called them "little white lies," suggesting a spectrum existed between honest and dishonest that hers were closer to honest, so not very bad. How we teach others by our example!

One of the items she sold were women's handbag crochet kits, which included all the materials and instructions necessary to make a handbag. She thought that while I was bedridden, she could teach me to crochet and I could make handbags as samples for the yarn stores and also sell them directly to individuals who might want them.

Well, I really took to this. I became very fast at crocheting and could do it without looking while watching TV. I made many different styles, selling primarily to stores. I would buy my own kits and materials and bill the stores directly for the samples I sold them. When in the hospital, I would display the bags on a table just outside my room. Made a few sales there, too—it did not matter to me that some might have been sympathy purchases!

What this whole activity did for me was incredibly good. It gave me a purpose and the therapy of handwork. It was creative and taught me more about a small business—a step beyond the paper route! I'm ever grateful to my grandmother to have done all this for me. It was a gracious gift of love. And, I made more than $3,000. Big money in 1956!

Discovering Jazz. I listened to pop music and rock and roll, like most other young people. I would often lay outside in the sun when I could use a walker, and listen to a small transistor radio. I enjoyed this music, but had no passion for it. After Leonard Mendoza left our life, or so I thought, my mother resumed going to bars and bringing men home for the night or for several nights. I do remember the phone ringing late at night when a man stayed over. I could hear my mom's end of the conversation. It was always Leonard Mendoza calling to taunt her about a man being with her. He would stalk the house at all hours. Even then, home didn't feel like such a safe place.

One of the men who stayed at the house for several days was a jazz piano player she met at a bar. He was a nice fellow who took time to talk with me. He introduced me to Schlitz beer, telling me that it had all the nutrition one needs for breakfast! I did not prefer the taste for breakfast. But, he did tell me about jazz piano and brought me a recording of Dave Brubeck. I still remember the tune. It was "On the Alamo" and I have never heard it since that recording. This was one of the first recordings by Brubeck—long before his classic, "Take Five." I was mesmerized.

There was this cool melody surrounded by fascinating musical departures that carried a faint thread of the theme, often building tension that was released by returning to the theme. It was magical to me. I could really go into the music. Lose myself there. I could connect with my deeply buried emotions.

I found a radio station that played a bit of jazz. That's when I first heard "Midnight Sun," written and played by vibraphonist

Lionel Hampton. I had never heard anything so beautiful, and it was deeply touching. I had tears whenever I heard it. I could express deep feelings with jazz; a necessary part of healing the whole self. For me, jazz is therapy! This was the first recording I ever bought. I asked my mom to get it for me.

Then I heard pianist Ahmad Jamal and was blown away by his composition and playing. I bought his first album: "At the Pershing." I especially loved his "Poinciana" and "But Not For Me." Ahmad Jamal has woven through our lives. Shirley and I saw him on our weekend honeymoon in San Francisco in 1963, and while living in Sacramento and later in Boston. My passion for jazz, especially piano jazz, grew from this man who cycled through my mom's bedroom. It was a gift, as it has helped me to feel, to connect with some of what I had to shut down in order to survive.

This passion finally led me to take jazz piano lessons starting at age 66. Today I play an arrangement of both "Midnight Sun" and "Poinciana" written for me by my piano teacher. I never get tired of them. My ability to play them touches me deeply. And by the way, as of this writing, Ahmad Jamal is still performing at his best and making CDs in his late 80's! Check him out…

My Lowest Moment—And Highest

My right leg had been in that chest-high cast for many months. Periodic x-rays revealed the bones had not healed as they should. The doctor decided to remove the cast, hoping that the extra external stress on the bone would stimulate and promote healing. I was not allowed to stand with my walker, but had to stay in bed and do some leg lifts. At the time, the cast had been off for just a week or two. As I lifted my right leg for some leg lifts, I felt a sharp pain and "crack" as the bone broke in the same place AGAIN!

I had been bedridden for a year, during which I was counting the days until healing would be complete enough for me to begin my metamorphosis to walking again. I knew my confinement was temporary and that the end was steadily drawing closer. Until now—when my leg broke... again.

I sunk as low as I had ever been or have been since. I hit bottom. A sense of black hopelessness enveloped me. I capitulated. I gave up. I knew that my human strength and endurance was just not enough. I had nothing left. This deep grief lasted a short time—an hour or so.

Then something happened that I can't properly describe. I suddenly felt weight lifting from me—a sense of weightlessness and the surrounding presence of comforting, uplifting light. It filled my consciousness. I was aware of nothing else. I heard no voices or singing or bells, but I suddenly had a deep and definite ***knowing*** that I was, and would be, alright. I became acutely alive! I was in awe of living and felt an indescribable peace.

This epiphany did not last long—it could have been several minutes or an hour. I didn't matter how long. That it happened is the wondrous thing. Nothing can explain what really happened. And, while the euphoria left, what remained was a deep knowing that I was not alone, that life is very good, and that I would be okay. I was touched by the Divine when my need was greatest. Imagine! I was overcome with a very humble sense of gratitude even when, to human sense, things looked pretty bad.

The best description of this was written by Mary Baker Eddy in her incredible book, *Science and Health with Key to the Scriptures*, where she says, "One moment of divine consciousness, or the spiritual understanding of Life and Love, is a foretaste of eternity."

Soon after this repeat fracture, the doctor performed bone grafts on both legs. But he cautioned in advance that if the bone grafts didn't take, nothing else could be done and I'd be an invalid thereafter. The bone graft involves taking pieces of bone from the front "wings" of the pelvis and placing them around each break. This greatly accelerated the healing. The next x-rays revealed rapid healing progress.

**My high school graduation photo.
(Check the hairdo!)**

After a few short months, I was able to move about with a walker. Then I was fitted with a brace on one leg and graduated to crutches. I could "walk" with crutches at good speed—as fast as anyone could actually walk. My arms and chest became very strong.

I finally resumed high school and could use my crutches to walk to and from Willow Glen High School, about 1.5 miles from home!

The Lawsuit. I don't know if we were approached by a lawyer or if Mom initiated contact. But, we retained a lawyer on a contingency basis to bring suit against the driver of the truck, and his insurance company, that turned over the double lines in front of us, causing the collision. My lawyer was a partner in a very successful trial law firm. He did a good job, as the case was difficult. The motorcycle I was on had knobby tires used for dirt tracks and were not good for stopping on pavement. That, plus reduced maneuverability with two people on the bike going fast, were obstacles to getting a good judgment. This was my first exposure to things legal.

I was awarded $3,000 after legal fees. I think I used much of it on cars, but did have some left for college, although I had no intention of going to college when I received this money. This exposure to the legal profession may have played a part in my later joining it.

Financing Mom's Marriage #4. While living in Willow Glen, Mom met Darrel Biggs. He worked as a lineman for the phone company. The lucky part for me was that he worked for Shirley's Dad, Al Haller, who was a construction foreman. Darrel had been married some time previously and had an estranged daughter. After dating for awhile, they decided to get married. Darrel was a gentle person who treated me well.

Although Darrel had a job and Mom operated a hairdressing business from our home, they were apparently both broke! Mom told me they needed a loan from me to go to Carson City, Nevada for a weekend to get married! I loaned her the money from my crocheting business. They did get married. I did get repaid. Can you imagine anything more goofy! That was a foretaste of the future.

When Darrel died in his late 70's, he left Mom destitute. He had been an alcoholic and died from that and severe emphysema. Except for Social Security, she received a small, lump-sum insurance payment which was used up in a few months. I provided the necessary financial help for her care as none of her three daughters had the resources to do so. But, Barbara provided selfless, on-site support for her, for which I'm so grateful.

Barbara. Barbie was born when I was 16 and still bedridden. She was a very cute baby who was loved and cared for. She was the apple of Darrel's eye. By the time Barb became a child, I had left home. So, we never had much of a relationship. It was only after she was married (a second time), had two boys and we had moved to Lake Tahoe after retirement, that we kept in touch and visited occasionally. Barb really stepped in to help care for Mom after Darrel died. While I provided necessary funds for Mom's care, Barb was the one who visited her regularly in her independent living and later assisted living facility. She took her to doctor appointments and shopped for the few essentials Mom needed.

Barb and her husband Currie had two sons, Sam and Jared. Because Shirley and I believe education is so important to success in life, we set up education trusts to help pay the cost of a four-year degree for each of the boys. But, they had to complete their studies before age 24 or forfeit the trust amount to a charity we chose. Sam was very devoted to his studies and worked while attending high school and college. He completed his degree and has moved on to graduate school. Jared had a different kind of success. He was indifferent about school and got hooked on drugs. His addiction continued for several years, despite the best efforts of his parents until a serious overdose occurred that got him to a recovery facility in Florida. Although he forfeited his education trust, he did recover and is successfully counseling and leading others to a better life.

Lynda. My full sister, Lynda, is two years younger than me. She had a truly difficult childhood. I was the only male around, and with the sympathy and attention that came to me through my physical travails, she took the brunt of Mom's screaming tirades. She was never really cared for, nor given any demonstrable love. She had no real father figure, either.

Lynda grew up in the shadows. She got a job, dropped out of high school, bought a car, and left home—all at 15! Within a couple of years, she married and was soon pregnant. I'm not really sure which came first. The marriage lasted but a few months. Her daughter was Tonya. Lynda and Tonya would challenge the world together. Some time later, Lynda met Joyce. They lived together in a lesbian relationship. Joyce had a son about Tonya's age. They were together for as long as 20 years, living in Hawaii and in Fremont. Lynda and I had very little contact. I recall visiting her once in Hawaii, once in Fremont and once in Reno.

Tonya married Harold Berlin in Las Vegas. Shirley and I attended the wedding. Harold has a large Hispanic family. He's a very good person. They have a truly wonderful boy and a girl and a stable relationship. So much for the anti-gay argument that gay parents cannot provide a healthy environment for raising children. Thanks to Tonya's initiative, we have been in touch and have enjoyed their several visits to our San Luis Obispo farm in recent years, as well as visits with us while at Tahoe.

Lynda and Joyce split up after Joyce found someone else. Lynda was later in touch with Donna, whom she knew before living with Joyce. They soon moved in together, living in Las Vegas. We talk by phone once or twice each year. We have not seen each other in person for many years. We have grown so differently that it is difficult to relate with so little in common. In some ways, Lynda has had the more difficult childhood.

Kathy. My half sister, Kathleen, never knew her father. He was Jack Ritter who committed suicide so grossly before she was born. She was born at the bleakest time in our lives. Kathy is nine years younger than me, so we have lived virtually separate lives. Home life was not so easy for Kathy, either. Like Lynda, she had to endure much of Mom's verbal tirades, especially since Lynda didn't stick around long to share the abuse. She too had no father to intervene and support her. Darrel came on the scene when she was around seven. But, as he had fathered his own daughter with Mom, Barb got most of his affection.

Kathy was about 16 when Shirley, Michelle, Lisa, and I lived in Sacramento. One weekend we made a trip to Reno to visit Mom, Darrel, Kathy, and Barb. Mom and Kathy were having serious trouble in their relationship. The poison between them was palpable. We believed something had to be done. The situation could not continue as it was. So, then and there, we offered, or insisted that Kathy return to Sacramento to live with us. Kathy quickly agreed. Mom merely acquiesced, perhaps secretly relieved.

The adjustment was difficult for Kathy. She continued high school nearby and began meeting some friends. Not all of them were best for her. We had hoped that a more positive, supportive environment would be enough. But, Kathy seemed to want independence from authority of any kind.

After about six months, Kathy insisted that she wanted to move in with a friend. This was difficult because we knew that if we said no, she would do it anyway. Returning her to Reno was not an option at that point. So she moved out. We kept in touch, but she had begun her own separate life.

A couple of years later, Kathy met Mark Maddy. He was a nice man: a very artistic, free spirit. He could have been called a hippie at the time. They were involved with drugs. Then they found the Church of Scientology and ultimately moved to the church's compound in rural Oregon. This experience was probably good for them, compared with the path they had been on. We visited them there just after their daughter Jocelyn was born.

My sisters and me (from left): Lynda, Mike, Kathy, Barb in the 1990s.

On several occasions, Kathy would phone me to plead for money. She explained that she desperately needed it to pay for Scientology classes or training. As difficult as it was to turn her down, I just could not do it. She sounded as though she had been coached in how to get the money. I could not understand how a member of a church could be required to pay so much (several hundred dollars) to the church in order to grow in that church. And they had worked very hard for the church while living at the church's compound for no more than a very small room and meals. Nevertheless, it was hard to say no.

They later moved from the church's compound to Portland where they had their son Colin. In order to help them buy a house and be independent, we loaned them $5,000. It was a lot for us at the time. A couple of years later, we decided to forgive the loan and freely gave it to them. Kathy and Mark later split up and divorced. Kathy moved to the Tampa, Florida area. Mark went elsewhere. Kathy and I talk by phone or email occasionally. She came to Reno to visit Mom every year or two. She still struggles to make her way on her own financially. Jocelyn is happily married. Colin spent much of his teen years with his Dad, but is now on his own.

When Mom entered the hospital the day she passed on, Kathy didn't hesitate to clear her schedule and get on a plane to Reno to support Barb and help with any final duties. She spent two days at our Tahoe condo, so we had a great time chatting and catching up on everything from family to religion. Her visit did strengthen our relationship.

Chapter 6

I Love Cars!

An Early Start Behind the Wheel

Now, nothing is particularly enlightening about me and cars. As I reviewed what I wrote, I realized that I devoted a lot of words to it. So, this is a section that you could skip without missing much!!

I love cars. Even before I learned to drive, at about age 12, I remember getting in a neighbor's pickup truck. Of course, I couldn't start it without the key. But, I could step on the starter. Yes, the starter pedal was on the floor. With the car in gear, it would slowly move as the starter turned the engine over. I would keep going until the battery died or I got caught, whichever came first. I did get busted when the owner figured out what I had been doing.

I finally learned to drive properly in our 1953 Ford station wagon. It had an automatic transmission. Then we got a 1950 Hudson that had a stick shift. I drove it whenever I could sneak it away, as I hadn't yet got a license. I would "speed shift" and try to "lay rubber." What a tough car it must have been, because it never broke. It is a wonder that the police never stopped me.

On crutches with my '41 Merc convertible.

The first car I owned was a 1941 Mercury convertible. I paid $120 for it. It had a loud exhaust and metallic blue paint. I would tinker with the engine and fix small things. I put long spring shackles on it and lowered it to about two inches off the ground in front. I thought it looked really cool, but it rode like a tank. Fortunately, I never got a flat tire. This is the car I had when I met Shirley. Her Dad was very unhappy that she would go out with someone with a car like that. So he forbid her to ride with me. But, we found ways around that.

My next car was very, very cool: a 1934 Ford two-door Victoria. It was raked with big rear tires that caused a front-to-rear slope.

It also featured shiny, black lacquer paint with a wide turquoise racing stripe down the middle, and a big Oldsmobile V8 engine. It was a fast car and looked great. A friend and I drove it all the way to Tijuana, Mexico and had the interior reupholstered in white naugahyde "tuck & roll." I had one of the coolest looking cars in high school.

My best friend, Jim Huntsinger, bought a 1934 Ford two-door sedan. He and I did a lot of work on it. We put four carburetors on its flathead V8 engine, high compression heads, and header exhausts. Jim had it painted a beautiful, rose-colored lacquer. We loved to cruise around in each of our cars together. They were definitely "hot rods" and very eye catching.

Shirley and I with my '34 Ford Victoria… Yes, whitewalls were the thing then!

While driving home one day in my '34 Ford, gazing at the gas gauge to see if I needed to add another 50 cents worth of gas, I didn't see the car ahead quickly slow down. I bumped into it, bending my perfect front grille. I put a small dent and scratch in the other car. But the driver, a woman named Edgerton, later claimed she had a whiplash neck. Whether she really did triggered much dispute. Our insurance agent alleged that although we had previously discussed coverage, it had not been made effective. I had to hire an attorney to sue the agent and the insurance company. I won the case and the insurance company had to pay the costs of the accident.

I was beginning to yearn for something different. When a fellow I knew expressed interest in trading his very clean 1956 Chevy Impala two door hardtop straight across, I jumped at it. It had a beautiful black lacquer paint job. I lowered the car a bit and added some very cool tires. Jim Huntsinger and I took another trip to Tijuana and had black tuck & roll upholstery installed throughout. It looked great.

I was then working part-time at Sam Fowler's garage and gas station. Once I proved my worth by pumping gas, Sam gradually showed me how to perform tune-ups, valve adjustments, brake jobs, etc. When things were slow and all was ship-shape, I could work on my car. One day I was doing some work on the carburetor, and while it was off the manifold, I dropped a nut or bolt down one of the intake ports. I didn't know it until I later started the engine, heard some bad sounds, and the engine ran very badly.

I took my car to a friend's house; he was an avid hot rod mechanic. I bought a Corvette engine short block and four-speed manual floor shift transmission. We installed all this in my Chevy. Wow, the results were exhilarating. That's when some hot rod friends convinced me that a drive to the Bonneville salt flats to watch the world land speed record trials would be a good way to break in my new engine. Four of us took the long but interesting trip.

The salt flats were indeed flat and big—a great place to see how fast anything with wheels would go. The star attraction was a very sleek machine of Mickey Thompson's with four big Pontiac V8 engines—one at each wheel. The goal was to break 300 miles per hour. They had mechanical problems and never quite got there. That was 1959. Now dragsters exceed 300 mph in a quarter mile and do it in a few seconds!! Incredible.

Some of the cars in my life:
- 1959 Austin Healey roadster while in college.
- 1956 VW bug. After the Healey in college—many miles to and from Shirley in Stockton at COP (later UOP).
- 1962 Austin "box"—an incredibly boring but practical car that we purchased when we were first married.
- 1964 Austin Healey—bought it new. What a wild and crazy thing we did and loved, until Michelle got too big to ride in her bassinet on the package tray in the back. We were driving from Napa to Shirl's parents house in Capitola in that boring Austin box. As we drove through San Jose, we saw the British Sports Car dealer sign and decided to have a look at their inventory. Well, they had the most beautiful, blue Austin Healey convertible. We had to have it immediately. I was the reluctant one, but Shirley was so convinced we should do it, I agreed. So, we traded in the Austin and drove on to Capitola in that wonderful new car.

That kind of impulsiveness was not like me. I didn't think it was like Shirley either, but this was the first of many wonderfully unlimited actions she would initiate that enhanced our lives. This was certainly one of the most exhilarating things I had ever done and it allowed me/us to jump outside "the box" more easily thereafter.

- 1965 Chevy Impala—bought used. Decent looking but practical, especially with two kids. It replaced the Healey. Most any car would be pedestrian following that.
- 1959 Porsche Cabriolet—our first second car. It fed my still latent car passion. I spent time and money on new paint, upholstery, and rebuilding the engine. I bought this car without Shirley's support. In fact, when I spent $1,500 to have the engine rebuilt, Shirl then spent $1,500 at Saks and showed me the credit card receipt and purchases to make the point!
- 1970 VW Camper Bus—We bought it while in Mill Valley. These were the hippie days and although we were not hippies, we were not out of place driving this. It replaced the Porsche and Chevy and we used it to trek our family across-country when we moved to Adrian, Michigan. We arrived in this small farm town in our hippie bus loaded with two kids, a Labrador retriever, baskets of special plants, and two cases of wine. We did get strange looks from the locals! We came to feel it might have been easier to have moved to a foreign country.

For the next 20-plus years, I drove boring company cars. Until "retirement." Then:

- 1996 Porsche 911 Carrera. This is (I still have it) a really sweet, fast car that loves to be driven aggressively. Shirley claims it as hers—now that she has mastered manually shifting through six gears. I guess she has some right to that, particularly since she urged me to get it. It has proven very practical for hauling young grandkids, thanks to no airbags in the back and higher, smallish seats with shoulder-strap seat belts.

One of my joys was taking a weekend performance driving course at a road racing track with a friend. After some class instruction and several laps following an instructor, we were set free to go as fast as we could around this 2.5 mile course. Talk about adrenalin! The joy of drifting out of a turn exactly right, and the terror of wondering where I'd end up when it didn't go quite right, was exhilarating.

I did spin out on a chicane when, doing about 90, I drifted a bit far to the edge and did all the wrong things: took my foot off the gas as I turned toward the center. The rear-heavy Porsche then took on a life of its own and spun 360 degrees for what seemed like forever while engulfed in screeching, smoking rubber. Once it all stopped and I discovered I had survived and hadn't hit anything, I proceeded to the pits where they checked all around to be sure nothing came loose. Then I immediately took off around the track a few more times at what I'm sure was a slower pace. Would I do it again? When can I go!?

The opportunity came three years later when a friend invited me to join him for a three-day Skip Barber racing school at Laguna Seca, near Monterey. This was an incredible experience—I drove their cars (tricked out Mazda 6 with racing tires, suspension, and roll cage). I was in a class of six with three instructors. We had many racing sessions of 25-30 minutes going flat-out around that legendary track where Formula One races used to be held. I learned a lot, never spun out, and was pretty darned fast. After going flat out on the track for 20-plus minutes, I'd be wrung out from the incredible focus required. I can't imagine what it takes to drive a Formula One car for nearly two hours on challenging tracks against 20 other F1 cars as the professionals do.

- 1959 Jaguar XK 150S—I've always had a dream of the perfect sports car to drive Highway 1—it was an old Jag roadster. I found it at the local British Sports Car garage in San Luis. It was bright red. I had chrome wire wheels put on it. It was a powerful car with a straight 8 engine with twin overhead cams and three carburetors. But, it was hard to steer and the clutch was very heavy. What turned out to be the big problem was that, other than the paint, the car was original. It had never been restored and needed it.

I found myself in the process of what I called "progressive restoration." Seemed like every time I took the Jag for a drive, I'd return, having to fix or replace some parts. Once while driving on 101 with Michelle, huge plumes of steam and water began gushing from the hood over the windshield. The radiator failed. More than once, I'd drive off to be towed back! I learned that the cost to fully restore it could never be recovered. So, I took it back to my friend at the British Sports Car garage to sell it. He did so, and at a price very close to what I paid (excluding all the progressive restoration costs).

- 1961 Porsche Cabriolet Super 90—After the Jag, I still wanted an old cool car, but a completely restored version. An old Porsche seemed right since we'd had one before and they have no radiator to leak nor electrical problems like that dismal Jag. I found the perfect Porsche online at a restoration shop in Costa Mesa that specialized in old Porsches. It had a complete frame-off restoration and looked sweet. It cost about what I got for the sale of the Jag and it has since tripled in value! I drive it regularly. I think it can drive itself to the post office in Avila, since that's mostly where it goes each week or so.

SECTION 4

The Value of Hard Work and Finding Love

CHAPTER 7

A Strong Work Ethic

Job Satisfaction

It seems like I have always worked—from picking fruit when 11 or 12, to having a daily paper route for nearly three years, then washing dishes or working at a gas station. I was always doing something to make money. Paying for my needs was important, but it was just part of my values to work—to do what was productive as I saw it.

Work was a way to have some mastery over my life, and it was satisfying to feel productive. I worked several jobs during high school and college. I was blessed with experiences and people that taught me more than the value of the money I earned. But, the money was indeed important as it was the way I paid the cost of: enjoying my cars; hanging out; going on dates; and buying stuff like clothes and the incidentals relating to college life. My grandmother was a big help with financing college tuition and helping me move on campus my first year at San Jose State.

Here are snapshots about some of these jobs:

The Car Wash. While in high school, I worked weekends at a local car wash. I did this for a year or so. I was proud that I had a regular job and some reliable income for my modest spending. I started vacuuming cars. It was very physical work with lots of bending while maneuvering the big vacuum hose and shaking out floor mats. I went home pooped.

After I had been working for a while, I was able to drive the cars from the vacuum station onto the conveyor that pulled the cars through the wash. I drove all kinds of cars and don't remember ever crashing any. But, I did occasionally burn a little rubber when the customer was not nearby!

Shirley would come by and park on the other side of the fence near my vacuuming station. This was during the time that her father would not permit her to see me. So, we stole some time together on each side of the chain link fence!! It is a very sweet thing in my memory.

Sam Fowler's Gas Station. While still in high school, I worked for at least two years at Sam Fowler's gas station. It had two pumps and a three-bay car repair garage with one hydraulic lift. Sam lived next door to the station. He was a piece of work. He must have been in his early 50's but looked like he was in his 70's. He was a beeraholic—he always wore a brown shop coat. Every day, he walked across the street kitty corner to the liquor store to replace his large bag of empty Pabst Blue Ribbon beer bottles with full ones. A bottle of beer was always open in the shop.

Sam never walked directly across the street because that is where his brother operated his own car repair garage. He would not dare venture that close. They hadn't talked with each other for many years. I never learned why. It must have been a major family feud with very long memories.

Sam was the original curmudgeon. He was gruff, opinionated, and very judgmental. But, he had a great deal of common sense and plain wisdom that is often missing in our "too smart" world. He didn't talk much. He had several old friends that would stop by and chat—and have a beer. Some of them drove old Ford Model A's of 1926 to 1930 vintage. Sam could fix whatever they needed.

I started just pumping gas, checking oil levels, and washing windows of customers. This was well before self-service, when $5.00 could fill your tank. Over the months, Sam taught me about keeping the books and recording the gasoline pumped. Over time, he allowed me to do some minor repair work, which he gruffly taught me. I could repair tires, change tires on rims, and do minor tune-ups. Eventually I would be doing brake jobs, valve adjustments, carburetor rebuilding, etc. When Sam decided I could handle the place while he went away for a few days I was thrilled—most of all by the trust this hard nosed old curmudgeon had placed in me. I learned from Sam that trust had to be earned. And, once earned, was something to be very proud of.

I believe that Sam grew to like me very much and I owe a lot to him for what I learned. I visited him at his station one day while I was attending San Jose State College (now San Jose State University). He was noticeably proud of me. His appreciation of my growth greatly boosted my self-confidence. Sam was another of the growing army of people who blessed me along my path and had a big hand in shaping my values and aspirations, as well as raising my thought about who I really was.

Other Jobs

Sam Ball's GasUteria—Yes, that was the name for this gas station. This Sam had no repair garage. He only pumped gas at a discount price. He had several pumps, and when cars arrived at each all at once, I would really have to hustle to dispense the gas, clean windshields, check oil levels, and collect the money. The best part about working here was that it was just two blocks from where Shirley lived, so it was easy to visit her and for her to drop by during slow times.

Washing Dishes—While in high school, I washed dishes at an upscale restaurant in Willow Glen called the Little Chef. It could be hard work, but I really loved working hard and fast and feeling a sense of accomplishment of getting a lot done. It always disturbed me to see how much food people left on their plates to be thrown out. I think about that when we eat out even now!

During college, I worked at The Old Bar B Que Pit. Located near my fraternity house, it was owned by the father of my good high school friend Bob Locke. Bob was a special friend. He had suffered with a hair lip and spoke with a definite lisp. Kids made fun of him. He didn't have any friends except me. We got along well. But he didn't go on to college, choosing to work at a steel company instead.

So, we drifted apart. I never knew anyone who could work harder than Bob. We both worked at his dad's restaurant and would have contests for who could wash dishes the fastest, peel the most potatoes, or chop the most celery. Bob usually won. The more he sweat and the faster he went, the happier he was. I remember us both laughing at being completely exhausted. He taught me the true joy and pride of really hard work for its own sake… to know the fulfillment of pushing past fatigue while doing something productive.

Bob's step dad, Glen, was very kind to me. He drove a cool MG roadster and was an amateur radio operator (a ham). He was very quiet, expected my best efforts, and always took an interest in my college work and job hunting prospects as I neared graduation. One perk of dishwashing that I never overlooked was the meal included during my work shifts. I still remember those great BBQ beef sandwiches and warm, deep-dish berry pies with ice cream. *Mmmmm.*

Almaden Vineyards and an Epiphany

Working here was a turning point. I had graduated from high school and decided I would rather work and make money than go to college. Heck, I really didn't know what I would want to study to become, anyway. My best friend, Jim Huntsinger, worked at Almaden Winery part time while in high school, then full time after graduation. His dad was the chief chemist there and helped me get the job.

We carpooled early each morning for the 15-mile drive to work. One of my first jobs was making up cardboard wine boxes. This meant opening the flattened boxes, folding the bottom flaps in, and using a big, air-powered stapler to secure the flaps closed. I had to be fast and worked with another older guy who had done this for years. I marveled at his effortless speed and could never match it.

Another job was stapling closed the full cases of wine as they came down the conveyor belt, and stacking them on pallets. This could get tense because I had to keep up with the speed of the cases coming at me. If something didn't go quite right for me, the cases would begin to stack up. If it got too bad, they had to stop the line and everyone would have to wait for me. The bosses did not like that.

One day I was told that I would be driving a forklift to move pallets of wine cases around, based on an order list. I was very proud of having this important job. However, I tended to drive a bit too fast. When rounding a corner too quickly with a stacked pallet of wine cases, the outer side of the stack would fall outward and down to the floor. My boss found me with a mop one too many times and I was demoted to loading railroad boxcars.

One of the really interesting parts of working in such a place amongst 50 to 60 other hourly employees is learning about other people's lives—namely, people who worked at repetitive tasks for an hourly wage for many years. With coffee breaks in the morning and afternoon and an hour lunch break, we had plenty of time to talk about things. I heard about what people did with their spare time, money, girlfriends, families, kids, etc. These were mostly nice people who worked hard and were reliable. They weren't very educated and watched a lot of TV.

Loading boxcars was very hard work. We drove a big flatbed truck loaded with cases of wine to a railroad siding where we'd stop beside a boxcar. We opened the boxcar doors and set up a long ramp with rollers from the truck into the boxcar. One guy sent cases down the ramp, and another would receive it in the boxcar. He or another guy stacked the case. We had to load the boxcar to the ceiling. That is a lot of 30-50 pound cases of wine!! The four or five guys I worked with loading boxcars were older than me and some had been doing this for many years. This physically demanding job required no thinking.

The epiphany: one day, my consciousness leaped ahead. We were all taking a morning break and chatting. The topic as usual was what they watched on TV last night and what was in their lunch. I suddenly saw what this really meant: *This will be ME in 15 years if I don't change course: At 35, I'd be loading box cars, paid by the hour, talking about what was on TV and feeling excited to talk about what was in my lunch box!!* That was when I decided I had better go to school so I could do something better than load boxcars.

I didn't yet know what that something would be, but that was not as important as moving along a path away from where I had been headed. I suddenly saw that it wasn't enough for me to simply work physically hard. I had to apply hard work in a direction that utilized my intellectual capacities as well. This was a major turning point for me.

My Best Friend

Unfortunately, that path departed from my best friend, Jim Huntsinger. He did not go for more education, but continued to work at Almaden Winery, got married, and had a family.

The last memory of doing something together was partying at Christmas time. We went to a couple of parties of other winery workers and drank a lot. We were in Jim's very cool 1960 Pontiac Bonneville, which he lowered. It looked great. It was wet and rainy. Jim was going too fast, lost control, and hit a tree. I don't know how we managed not to get seriously hurt, as his car was badly damaged and seatbelts were not part of cars yet.

Jim never seemed the same after that. It was like he was overwhelmed with guilt for having wrecked his car, for being drunk, and for every other "sin" he had committed. He became withdrawn and spent his spare time with the girl he later married. We did not see each other again until 15 years later when we lived in Mill Valley. I found that he and his family were living in Napa where he was the winemaker at a small winery. We visited them in Napa and they visited us in Mill Valley. We had nothing in common and found it difficult to relate; we had followed such different paths that our previous relationship couldn't bridge. We had no further contact. I miss what we had as friends so long ago. Change can be difficult, but I'm grateful for what we shared together back then.

CHAPTER 8

Shirley: The Greatest Blessing of a Blessed Life!

How We Met

"Do you want to come with us to the lake?" asked Darrel, my new stepfather. I was just getting up in the morning and was still on crutches from the accident.

"I don't think so," I said.

"We're meeting Al Haller there and he has two daughters and a beautiful Chris Craft ski boat," he said.

"Okay," I responded. Al was Darrel's boss as foreman of a phone company construction crew on which Darrel worked.

Al Haller did, indeed, have two daughters. When I met Shirley Haller, I was smitten. I was 16 and she was 15. She and the others water skied while I watched. Shirley was beautiful. She seemed shy, and was a good skier. We talked. It might have been the following day that I called her. Next, I drove to her house and we visited. That's how the courtship began. Shirley still claims that she believed, on that very day at the lake, she would meet the man she would marry!

We went to the movies and restaurants, and on rides in my beloved 1941 Mercury convertible, my first car. Her Dad soon forbid her from riding in my car, as it was loud and looked dangerous at just two inches off the ground. Not long after that, he forbid Shirley to see me at all. I'm not clear as to his reasons. He knew my Mom through Darrel and likely did not approve of my Mom's lifestyle or values, so he had trouble seeing how I could be any better. He told Shirley that I would never amount to anything—that I might be a milkman or postman at best. He predicted that I'd be a cripple by age 40!

Over time, Al began to accept me and later respected me some. When I started getting successful, like rising higher than him in the phone company, becoming a lawyer, then a business executive, he began to think I was acceptable. Ironically, he started to take some credit for my success; he believed that his open predictions of my failure made me work even harder to prove him wrong. After we married, I learned to respect some of his qualities, like really hard work and discipline, standing strongly for what he believed, and being financially responsible. He was a quite opinionated and dogmatic fellow, but deep down, he had a very soft heart.

Forbidding us to see each other certainly made our relationship all the more interesting, even if challenging. Shirley drove to see me when I was working; usually with her sister, Terry. She parked behind the chain-link fence next to the car wash where I worked. She also drove to Sam Fowler's gas station where I worked while attending Willow Glen High.

I also remember visiting her at her grandmother's home in the hills above Los Gatos. What a gracious woman she was! She provided such wonderful support to Shirley and did not judge me harshly. I think she trusted Shirley's judgement! She was Shirley's exposure to Christian Science, which later had such an important healing role in our lives.

Shirley's High School Junior Prom.

Shirley has always seen the best in me. She knew I was capable of higher aspirations than I did. For example, when I finally did get to college and had sights on being a shop teacher, she insisted that I could do much more than that. She was right, but I was crushed that she didn't support my lesser goal. Shirley has always pushed me beyond my "limits"—she's the one who got us to buy that cool new Austin Healey on impulse, take sailing lessons, learn to scuba dive, learn to windsurf, buy the bigger boat, etc. What a blessing to my life. I can only hope that I've added more to her life than I've taken.

CHAPTER 9

Travel

The Trip of a Lifetime and a New Perspective

While in high school, my grandmother promised me and my sister that if we did not smoke, she would give us $300 or a trip to South America—our choice—when we graduated from high school. Well, I did smoke some. I never became addicted and usually smoked when someone I was with smoked or I could bum a cigarette. Being without cigarettes never bothered me. I don't know if my grandmother's offer kept me from being a smoker, but I always felt a little guilty when I did smoke. Maybe that was enough! So, when I graduated, I chose the South America trip. I don't know if Lynda ever collected money, because I know she never went to South America, but she never graduated from high school, either.

My grandmother's sister Dorothy married a Spaniard she met in college in the United States. Alfredo became a doctor and they moved to Lima, Peru. They had previously visited the States and I had met them and their two sons; one was about my age. I headed to Lima, but not alone. My Grandmother was going with me by freighter ship from Los Angeles to Peru.

The voyage was magical. We joined six other passengers, having our meals with the officers. With very little to do on the long ocean passages, we read, roamed the ship, and watched the ocean. I got to know several crewmembers and had interesting conversations with them about all sorts of things. One of my favorite things was to go to the bow at night and watch the stars and phosphorescence in the water made by the bow wave. It seemed that I could think much better here. The magic never left me as I loved it even more, years later, during many ocean passages on my own sailboat.

I think the voyage took more than two weeks. We made stops at Panama, Buenaventura, Columbia, and Guayaquil, Ecuador. The ship unloaded and took on cargo. This was long before containers. The cargo, in boxes, pallets, or barrels, was loaded into nets. Onboard cranes lifted them from the ship to the dock and vice versa. It was a slow, but interesting, process. I wandered ashore and walked around these very foreign lands with all the sights, sounds, and smells of a new adventure. I began to know how big, wonderful, and varied the world was, and that it was not a scary place.

The Calderons: cousins Paul and Peter,
Aunt Dorothy, and Uncle Alfredo.

My great uncle and aunt lived in a big house surrounded by high walls enclosing beautiful gardens. They had a maid and gardener who lived on their property. They lived a gracious life and my uncle was a most cultured, kind, and gracious man. If classes of people exist, then he was of the highest. But, he was a purposeful man who could be demanding. He was a well respected doctor for whom the waters seemed to part before him wherever he went!

I remember all of us going into the city to an obscure Chinese restaurant in a run-down area. The restaurant was called the "Chifa"—odd that I can remember the name after 50 years! He paid a man to watch his car while we were in the restaurant. Inside, my uncle took charge. He seated us, then set about to personally wash the dishes we were to eat from! Then he told the staff what we were having to eat. He even dished it out. The food was wonderful, especially the sweet & sour items.

I had been away from home four weeks now and I missed Shirley very much. I wrote her everyday. But, the mail was very slow, so I didn't get many of her letters. I also missed my car, but not as much as Shirl.

My grandmother arranged for us to visit Machu Picchu. That was quite an adventure in 1959, as it wasn't a major tourist destination then and wasn't easy to access. Our flight was on a propeller-driven plane that was not pressurized. Flying high over the Andes Mountains at 25,000-plus feet, we had to breathe oxygen through tubes at each seat because the plane was not pressurized.

We landed in Cuzco, the ancient capital of the Incas. Cuzco was like being in a different world. The sites and people were wonderful. The bright colors of their clothing and the history locked in the old buildings and stone streets were fascinating. My only problem was nausea and headaches from the altitude. I felt better after a couple of days.

The trip from Cuzco to the ruins of Machu Picchu was by a railroad bus! We actually rode in a bus that had train wheels. To stop, the driver cramped the wheels into the tracks because they had to get rid of the brakes to fit the train wheels. He really couldn't stop, but could slow down a bit, as was demonstrated when we came around a turn and nearly hit a cow standing on the tracks. The 60-mile trip was mostly along the Urubamba River and past small huts and villages and people with mouths stained red from chewing cocoa leaves. It was beautiful.

When we arrived at our destination, we climbed onto the back of a pickup truck, which crossed the river and climbed a narrow, steep dirt road with a series of switchback turns. At the top, I was suddenly greeted with the most incredible sight I had ever seen. I was looking out over terraces of stone walls, steps, and paths of an entire ancient town set atop a high, narrow mesa. As I wandered around, I saw how many of the huge stones were cut in jigsaw shapes and fit together so tightly that a knife blade could not fit between them. How could they have done this? It was all such a marvel. It is no wonder that Cuzco and Machu Picchu have become such popular tourist destinations today—and much easier to access now!

Another wonderful trip we took was the narrow gauge train to Huancayo. It was the highest scheduled railway in the world. It went by the many tin mines of the country and had to gain altitude at times by using switch-backs. This means the train climbed to the end of the track, stopped, switched the rail behind it, then backed up the next section of track to its end, then stopped and threw the switch now ahead of it, climbed further, and so on.

I loved to ride on the platform outside, between the cars as we chugged our way through narrow canyons, tunnels, and mountainsides. Near the summit, around 15,000 feet, a man came through the cars with a large inflated, black fabric balloon-like bag. It had a spigot for people to take oxygen! We were so high that it was exhausting to walk but a few steps. But, what an adventure.

I was in Peru about a month. It was a life-changing trip in that I was immersed in a completely different environment than I had ever known. It gave me a subtle sense of possibilities. I came to know people who actually lived on a completely different plane than anyone I had known. And, I made a connection with my Uncle Alfredo. I think he saw something in me that I didn't. I felt that he respected me. This really meant a lot because he was a really special man. I only wished I could have spent more time with him. He was another helping hand along my life's journey. I have so very much for which to be grateful.

Chapter 10

Education

A Student's Life

Not long after my epiphany that an education could be my path away from a mind-numbing life of physical labor, I enrolled at San Jose City (Junior) College. Having enjoyed my high school drafting class, I decided that drafting would be my major. I took the basic English, history, and math classes. But, it wasn't long before I realized that a job of drafting meant long hours of sitting glued to a big drafting desk doing pretty tedious stuff. I decided that I needed to go in a more creative and interesting direction.

The next semester, I decided on Industrial Design. It includes the designing of everything from packaging to furniture to small appliances. I liked the variety and creativity of it. But, I was sadly lacking the artistic talent to draw and color renderings of designs. Most of the other students were really good artists. I also realized that the creative process wasn't where I was very comfortable or talented. Even today I wouldn't dare deviate from the recipe when cooking, and I have a really tough time departing from the written music when trying to play jazz piano.

By this time, I had a year of Junior College and, encouraged by Shirley, was ready to transfer to San Jose State College. A bachelor's degree was clearly more valuable to my future than an Associate in Arts degree. But I had no clear sense of what my major should be. I decided on Industrial Arts. I would be a teacher of woodworking or metal working or whatever shop was in high school. I figured I was good with my hands and got along with young people, so this might be a good direction.

I enrolled as a sophomore at SJS as an Industrial Arts major. It wasn't long before Shirley suggested that she would prefer not to marry a shop teacher. She thought I could do much better than that.

Okay, but like what?

I'm not sure what thought process was used to get there, but I decided to major in Industrial Relations & Personnel Management. It's basically a business degree. A business major, then as probably now, was like the default major for many who don't know exactly what they really want to do. Nevertheless, I did have a strong sense for the importance of human resources and good relations between employees and management. At least I was specializing in a subset of the general business major.

The best thing I got from this major was being able to learn from and be advised by Dr. Pete Zidnak, a professor in Labor Relations. Dr. Zidnak was more a philosopher and idealist than a teacher. I'm sure he was also a communist. But, he made me think more deeply about big things than anyone before. I remember taking a course from him called Wage and Salary Administration. He asked us to read the book, but spent class time talking about social issues, labor justice, and philosophy. He had us write essays on various subjects with little direct relevance to Wage and Salary Administration. One such essay was to write on "which is more important: property rights or human rights?" Dr. Zidnak made a lasting imprint on my values regarding the nature of employment, business, and critical thinking. They stood me well as I progressed in business.

During my senior year, Dr. Zidnak encouraged me to do an internship. He helped arrange one for me at Goodwill Industries. Between himself, the manager of Goodwill, and I, we crafted a project that involved a sort of time and motion study of the Goodwill workers' job elements with the purpose of better estimating workload and personnel needs.

The manager at Goodwill was a very cool guy—smart, professional, and compassionate. He was also a "bohemian," someone who is deeply philosophical, lives in accord with his values, and places little importance on material things or others' opinions. Unlike later hippies, bohemians didn't necessarily "drop out" or openly rebel. Here was a kind and effective man who made little money, but was very engaged and passionate about helping others. He made a big impression on me and influenced my own values.

Goodwill Industries is a sheltered workshop, meaning they take in people with social, behavioral, or economic challenges and are exempt from certain employment requirements like minimum wages in order to help them learn life skills. They give them structure, while teaching basic job skills, what a job requires, and how to function in society. Since I was on the floor with them, describing and timing their work elements, I got to know them. I was very much an authority figure who was carefully inspecting what they were doing and using a stopwatch! This required me to apply all the diplomacy, people skills, and compassion that I had, and then some.

I learned a great deal about relating to people in a work setting. I also gained huge admiration for the manager who chose to spend his career helping people who were in such need. Here was a good, very capable man devoting his talents to helping people, not his bank account. As I got to know him, it became clear that his real income from what he did was not measured in dollars. Here was another big lesson I learned early along my path. Fulfillment comes in many significant ways that cannot be measured by money or status.

Fraternity Life

During my first year at San Jose State, I lived on campus in a dorm. My grandmother paid for this, bless her heart. Even though I could have lived at home and commuted, she thought it would enhance my college experience. She probably also thought it best for me to get away from home, although things had stabilized with Mom's temperament since she had remarried again and Lynda had moved out. This was my first experience living away from home, aside from extended trips or visits. I enjoyed dorm life, although I didn't like the constant activity and noise. I had two different roommates who were pleasant enough.

During spring semester, a friend encouraged me to "rush" a fraternity. I attended several rush parties where one meets some of the brothers of that particular fraternity. They sized up the attendees. I seemed to connect best with Sigma Chi. I was selected to pledge, which meant that I would attend pledge meetings, learn about the fraternity, and be subservient to the brothers. I was one of about 15 new pledges.

I decided to move from the dorm to the fraternity house. That was a mistake. My room was just inside the front door and near the phone. I was expected to answer the phone by the third ring, no matter when it rang. I was also required to do whatever chore a brother needed done, and I was conveniently located!

This situation led to sleep deprivation and insufficient studying. I may have lasted two months, then decided to live at home until

I was finished being a pledge at the bottom of the heap. Hell week was certainly that! One week before school started, we pledges were subjected to long hours of hard work on the house and grounds. We became dead tired and would be startled awake in the middle of the night to do exercises and more work. I don't think we got more than three or four hours of sleep per night for a week. But we experienced no direct physical abuse.

At the end of the week, we went on a quest of sorts followed by a ceremony transforming us from pledges to fraternity brothers. The bond that grew between all of us pledges was predictably very strong. We became good friends and remained so some years after graduation. Two of them were in our wedding party when Shirley and I married. Sadly, we lost contact after a few years.

I moved back to the fraternity after becoming a brother and stayed until I graduated. Life was much better now that new pledges had arrived, and I wasn't one of them! I don't regret the fraternity experience. The values represented are good. Although I didn't really enjoy the regular beer-drinking party scene, I did value the bond I shared with all of the fraternity brothers. This sense of belonging was what I sought most of my younger life and found in a more constructive way in Sigma Chi.

Regular Trip to Stockton

Shirley attended College of the Pacific, now University of the Pacific. Except for about a year during which we dated others, we were a steady couple. During our last year in college, we were engaged. So, I made the two-hour drive frequently and at all hours in my tired, old Volkswagen beetle.

These visits were difficult because we were very much in love and our time together was fleeting. I usually stayed at the Delta Upsilon fraternity house where one of the brothers was the boyfriend of one of Shirley's sorority sisters. Shirley was a Delta Gamma. It's a coincidence that 15 years later, I would graduate from UOP's law school—McGeorge in Sacramento.

Shirley and the college graduate beside his '59 Austin Healey.

Graduation

I graduated mid-year, after cutting six months off the normal four-year degree program, including my year at junior college. This was because I took summer school classes and usually carried a heavy class load, despite working part-time. I was very motivated to graduate because Shirley and I planned to marry after my graduation. As it turned out, we waited an extra six months after my commencement, until she was about to graduate after the following winter semester.

I graduated "With Distinction" and "Departmental Honors" because of good grades—a 3.2 GPA overall and a 3.5 GPA in my major. Not bad for one who had been asked to leave San Jose High and attend a trade school, and hadn't even intended to go to college. But, once I decided to complete college, I became very focused on doing it. Our plan to marry only after graduating was a serious motivator.

Forming Values

Today I often contemplate how one's values are formed. Maybe it's because I'm close to my grandkids, and I see their values developing. This makes me wonder, "How I can contribute in the best way?" It's also my concern for today's American values that seem to be slipping more and more into a mentality of entitlement, victimhood, and, "What's the government going to do for me?"

Of course, this story of my earlier life is very much about how my values were formed. I've had opportunities to develop values of hard work and learn about business that kids today just don't have. For example:
- Working all day picking fruit. Where are the orchards that are a bike ride away today? And what would today's child labor laws say about that, anyway?
- Having the small business of a paper route. I haven't seen a paperboy delivering papers on his bike for decades.
- Learning to provide service with a smile by pumping gas.

Gas stations have been self-service now for decades, too! There's still dishwashing, but I'd bet even that's gotten pretty automated.

My work ethic was also influenced by my Grandmother, who was a business woman all her life. She and my Grandfather owned and operated clothing stores for decades. After their divorce and the sale of their stores, she sold yarn to stores on the west coast for a yarn manufacturer.

Once, I joined her for several days on a business trip as she made her sales calls. She worked hard. Despite her mean streak, she could be incredibly charming, especially to clients and guests or anyone she wanted to impress. I think I learned that it was somehow okay to be mean, so long as I knew I could be nice later! So, what I learned from her wasn't all good.

My hard work ethic continued after college when Shirley and I managed 40 duplex units while working for the phone company, buying and refurbishing duplexes in my "spare time," attending law school at night, and managing cable TV systems while competing for franchises to wire communities.

Section 5
Marriage, Family & Career

Our engagement photo.

Chapter 11

MARRIAGE—finally!!

The Wedding

Although I graduated in May, Shirley didn't graduate from UOP until the following February after her student teaching. Though we had agreed to marry after we graduated, we figured that December would be close enough. So, on December 22, 1963, we were married in the Methodist church in Santa Clara after going together, except for a one-year hiatus, for six years!

The wedding pair.

Two of my fraternity brothers, Mike Ryan and Manny Cordova, and Shirley's brother, Bud Haller, were best men. That I had a Mexican "brother" was a fitting connection to my past. It was a beautiful wedding.

Our "honeymoon" was that weekend. After the ceremony, we drove to San Francisco and stayed in the Sheraton Grand Hotel on Market Street. The hotel is still there and the huge, stained-glass dome over the big dining room is as spectacular as ever. We stayed in the bridal suite, I had flowers and champagne in the room. We were really living!! After dinner at Trader Vic's, we saw Ahmad Jamal play at the Jazz Workshop. Amazingly, he is still playing well in his 90s!

Our wonderful weekend was almost ruined when I received a surprise call in the room the morning we were departing. It was my grandmother, asking me to come to the lobby! She was there and wanted to pay for our room. I would not accept it. It felt like such an awful intrusion into our special time. I didn't want her in the lead as we began our new life. I had to deal with her again on this issue of her importance later in our young married life. We then drove to our new home in Napa: a nice, small, one-bedroom apartment. My first job was there and Shirley commuted to UOP in Stockton to complete her last semester and student teaching.

FIRST JOB OUT—A Career for Life!

In those days, one normally began work for a large company and stayed until retirement. It was rare to leave a management job in a large company for a new job elsewhere, as is so common today. Security was important and job mobility was more limited then. So, it was natural for me to choose larger companies to interview when they came to campus.

I interviewed for Sears, Aerojet General, and Pacific Telephone. The phone company had an accelerated management program that was highly selective, but generally assured its participants to achieve district-level (third level) management within five years. After a series of tests and multiple interviews, I was offered a job in this Management Achievement Program (MAP). I took the job, which started with a month of training at their Sacramento headquarters.

My first position was Safety Manager for the Northern California Plant Division headquartered in Napa. My job was to measure safety performance and develop safety programs for the six outside plant districts of the division. This took me all over Northern California. It was challenging in that it was a "staff" job, meaning that I had no direct authority over anyone. I did get to work with and know many excellent managers in the process, and developed safety tracking programs.

About six months into the job, I was given responsibility for "G.O. 95 Compliance." I had two employees who drove around the division, taking sample measurements of clearances of phone wires over the ground and from power cables. I prepared reports for the relevant district managers so they could take corrective action as required. It was my first experience managing anyone. I learned that it was not so simple!

My next position with the phone company was as Chief Switchman, managing a central office in Petaluma. Now, my degree was in Labor Relations. I'd had no technical, mechanical, or electrical training. Yet, here I was, just a year out of college, in charge of the phone company's switching office in Petaluma!! I remember walking into this huge, 20-foot-high cavern of a building full of mechanical switching equipment from floor to ceiling, hearing all manner of mechanical chatter with bells, buzzers, and alarms sounding. Eight "switchmen," each averaging 15 years with the phone company, kept the switching office running.

I was their boss!! I soon was given six weeks of training in how to repair and adjust a step-by-step switch as the bulk of the phone switches in use were then called; I also learned how to read a basic electrical schematic diagram. But, that did little to qualify me to operate this complex switching office.

The big lesson here was that I didn't have to know how to operate the equipment, but to manage and prioritize the activities of these men who did know how. That required that I gain their respect by respecting them, listening carefully to them, and responding to their needs. If I failed at that, they could have sunk me before I even knew it happened. This was keen motivation to learn and apply what I could about leadership and managing people.

Our First Attempt at Owning Income Property

While we lived in Petaluma, we bought a very old house made over into four apartment units. The seller took a mortgage and down payment from us. To manage the place, we selected a nice elderly lady, Mrs. Ruckrigl, who lived there. We learned a lot about renting apartments, tenants, collecting rents and all the maintenance required of an old building. Its location was central in town, so it had good, long-term potential. But, after moving from Petaluma to Santa Rosa, then to Sacramento, we had difficulty keeping on top of it. And, it became a financial problem as vacancies and maintenance made it difficult to meet our payments and expenses. Our mortgage from the seller was non-recourse, meaning that if we defaulted, his remedy was solely to take the building back.

As hard as it was to admit failure and lose the money we'd invested, we gave the property back to the seller, thus ending our first attempt at income property ownership. Fortunately, later experiences were more successful.

Michelle is Born!

Shirley was pregnant with Michelle while in Petaluma, where we had a nice apartment from which I could walk to the Central Office. After about nine months on this job, I was moved to Santa Rosa, where I managed repair service at the Plant Service Center downtown. I had about 15 employees: repair service clerks who took trouble calls from customers, and deskmen who would test and analyze problem phone lines for the outside repairmen.

I took the bus to and from work. One day, a small, very cute, long haired, floppy-eared dog found Shirley while she waited for me in the park next to the bus stop. It seemed this dog came to bless us. She and Shirley met me every evening at the park when I got off the bus. Then we'd play hide and seek with "Fred," who would tear around the park in play. We chose "Fred" because that was how I playfully referred to our unborn child. Better to lay that on our dog than Michelle! We had Fred many years until she was run over by the milkman in Sacramento. That was a sad day, but Fred was getting very old and grumpy and departed this life very quickly. The milkman felt bad.

We moved to Santa Rosa while Shirley was pregnant. We lived in a duplex in a complex of 12 buildings with 24 units. We met and hit it off with the owner of the complex, who was looking for someone to manage them. He offered the job to us. So, in exchange for free rent, we collected rent, showed units to prospective tenants, and handled repair problems. Shirley did the bulk of this work. We learned more about owning and operating rentals.

Shirl began having a few labor pains, though irregular and spread out. A few earlier false alarms had occurred, and this was still two to three weeks before the due date. So, I went to work standing by the phone. Within a couple of hours I got the call!

Michelle was coming. Just 10 minutes from home, I arrived in a flash. Our car then was that beautiful Austin Healey roadster. Great, except it was low to the ground and rode very stiffly, and we needed to get to our doctor at the hospital in Petaluma. It was a rough, 20-mile drive that exacerbated Shirley's contractions. We made it. Michelle was born a few hours later. These were the days when the father waited in the waiting room, smoking and pacing the floor. Such a different time than when I was right there so many years later with my daughters Michelle and Lisa for the home births of each of their children. (Grandson Christopher's started at home, but finished in the hospital).

Michelle weighed less than five pounds. Although healthy, it was policy to keep premature infants in the hospital for several days until they were confident enough to release them. She was so very tiny—our baby could fit in the palm of my hand! But, she was the most beautiful and miraculous little person I'd ever seen.

Shirley's mother came to help for a few days while we got used to the routine. When Michelle was a month or two old, I remember driving with her in her little bassinet—which was a large basket—placed on the package tray behind the front seats of the Austin Healey. That worked fine, but we knew those days were numbered. But, we managed this way until we moved to Sacramento when we replaced the sports car with a proper family car—a Chevy Impala.

That's where we bought our first duplex. We lived in one side, which had two bedrooms, so Michelle had her own room.

More Rental Property

We moved to Sacramento because my job changed from managing Santa Rosa repair service to joining the Northern California Plant department budget staff. This was a pretty boring job of working with numbers, making projections, analyzing budget results, etc. I had no employees.

We decided to buy a duplex, which was walking distance from my office. It required very little down payment. The plan was to fix up the property, raise rents to increase the property value, and sell it. My plan was inspired by a book about how to build wealth by investing in rental property. After getting well along with painting, landscaping, and other minor improvements, the duplex next to ours came on the market.

We bought that one, too, and began making similar improvements. We were able to increase rents, which covered our two mortgage payments and expenses with our rental income. I did all this work on the properties while continuing my job at the phone company.

After about two years of owning these two duplexes, I learned of two more duplexes for sale. They were further out and in a less desirable area, but the price was low and the general condition was good. I thought they had good potential. So, we bought them and I commenced the usual sweat equity investment.

We owned these two duplexes for less than two years when we began looking for a house for our growing family. We found a newly built three-bedroom house in a very good area that the owner/developer was willing to trade for the two duplexes we most recently bought. It was a perfect arrangement. So, after living for three years or so in a small duplex, we had all the space we could want: three bedrooms, a two-car garage, and a large, unlandscaped yard. More work for us!!

Marriage: The Work Is Worth It!

Shirley and I married in San Jose on December 20, 1963. So, as I write this, we've been married for more than 55 years. How can that be? As we had been mostly together for six years before marriage, we've been married longer than some people live! When asked if it gets easier with time, I say no, the issues simply change. For me, it has been about commitment to Shirley and our marriage. I love Shirley more today than ever. My sense of love has evolved and deepened, as has our relationship.

Commitment! It was several years after the day of our marriage that I can say I made it unconditional. Sure, as newlyweds I harbored no idea of ever having any other relationship. Then, as the challenges of living as an individual and as a couple emerge, the depth of commitment is tested. I had no models of good marriages. I wasn't good at giving or being thoughtful to others. My personal communications were lousy.

When the heat of an argument increased, my impulse was to fade out—to run. Shirley would doggedly pull me back. Her perseverance in keeping us working through issues, no matter how stubborn I was, is one of the most important reasons for the success of our marriage. She took much more responsibility for our relationship than I did. She shouldn't have had to. But, I'm so grateful she did!

Our relationship hit new lows in Sacramento. Michelle and Lisa were maybe six and four. Shirley made an appointment with a marriage counselor: Dorothy Jayne. I very reluctantly went and did not enjoy the sessions. I think I began to understand intellectually that a good relationship and all that it took was a choice. The commitment thing! I believe Shirley kept seeing Dorothy after I decided I'd spent enough time at it. She was committed to continuing to grow personally, even if the growth of our marriage was stunted, despite her best efforts.

It's difficult to identify exactly when my commitment became unconditional. I knew that starting a new relationship with anyone else would simply result in having to deal with the same and probably more issues, just with someone new. I knew that physical attraction naturally declines over time. This knowledge was intellectual. The depth of my commitment to Shirley grew through the challenges we faced together, as well as my growing appreciation of the limitless support she gave me and difficulties she endured on my behalf. I'm reminded of the many homes she has made with our multiple moves, my law school regimen, raising our daughters largely without me, our Santa Cruz experience, and so on.

Chapter 12

Wife, Mother, Grandmother

Choice: Grandmother Versus Wife

I made a pivotal decision in my growing commitment to Shirley earlier in our marriage. We were living in the first duplexes we owned in Sacramento when my grandmother came to visit for a day or two. Shirley had written a letter to someone that she left on our bedroom dresser. It contained her remarks about how she did not look forward to my grandmother's visit and how hard it was to have her around. All true.

Well, while we were away from the house, my grandmother did some snooping and found what Shirl had written about her. When we returned, she was seriously pouting, then took me aside to tell me how awful Shirley was to write such mean things about her. She demanded an apology. I talked with Shirl about what my grandmother found and her reaction. It was clearly wrong for her to have snooped among our personal things. For Shirley to apologize for writing the truth in a personal letter not intended for her would be wrong.

I had no question in my mind about this. So, no matter how frightening it was to confront my strong-willed, controlling grandmother, I told her that she was very wrong to invade our privacy as she did, and that she would not be receiving an apology from Shirley. She told me how hurt she was and that she would not be staying any longer. I did not add my apology, nor did I urge her to stay. I don't remember any later fallout from this, although things were chilled for some time. I felt to my core that I had done the right thing. I was acting on my commitment.

My Mother

As an adult, I did not have much of a relationship with my mother. When we lived in Sacramento for eight years while Michelle and Lisa were little girls, Mom rarely took the time to drive just two hours from Reno to see them. I can count her visits on the fingers of one hand. Even then, her primary reason for the trip was to shop at Lane Bryant, "the fat lady's store," as she called it. My being a grandfather now makes it all the more incredible that her only grandchildren meant so little to her. But, that's how she related; she demonstrated isolation and I learned to mimic it.

We did visit her in Reno every two to three years to maintain some degree of connection. As we moved to Michigan and Boston, we visited briefly by phone on occasion. Mom had trouble speaking on the phone for more than about two minutes; she would get very anxious to hang up. Even after I retired to Tahoe, we only visited her and Darrel every three to four months. Darrel had emphysema, which caused great difficulty breathing, especially at the higher altitude of Tahoe. He was a real stick-at-home kind, so that suited him anyway. The only time I remember him at Tahoe was when Lisa, then Michelle, were married there.

Darrel suffered increasingly from alcoholism and emphysema. He never stopped drinking or smoking heavily. He died from this in 2002 at age 80. Mom was in fairly good physical and mental health until his death. Thereafter, we moved her from their mobile home to an apartment where she had no yard or maintenance chores. But, she soon began to get increasingly confused during daily activities. Bless Barbara who kept close watch on her and provided regular attention.

After a year or so in the apartment, it was clear that Mom needed to be where she didn't have to cook or clean and had some easily available activities. After Barb and I did some research, we moved her to an independent living facility where she had a small room and bathroom, sink, refrigerator, and microwave. This worked well for about four years. She took advantage of the games and other activities and kept physically active by walking.

One day I got a call from the manager, who said that she was requiring more and more attention and was becoming increasingly confused and agitated. He said we had to move her to an assisted living facility that provided closer supervision and help with her medication. He recommended a place nearby. Barb and I checked it out and agreed that it would suit her well, since it specialized in dementia and Alzheimer's care.

Any money Mom had was depleted by the time she moved into the independent living facility in 2004. Darrel left virtually no savings. They had very little equity in their mobile home and their cars had little value. Mom got a lump sum payout of about $25,000 from his Telco pension. Her Social Security income was about $900 per month. The $25,000 was gone within two years of Darrel's death. So, the difference between her monthly living expenses and Social Security was mine to pay, as no one else in the family had the resources to help.

This difference was $4,000 to $6,000 per month. This outlay continued until 2009 when I was able to move her to the only Medicaid-qualified nursing facility with dementia care in Northern Nevada. It was in Carson City. Since she was destitute and needed nursing care, she qualified for admittance. It was a locked-down facility where elderly patients had needs at every level imaginable. Mom got increasingly confused, but always knew who I was and carried on with a good attitude and a sense of humor.

One afternoon in 2011, I received a call from Barb that Mom had been taken to the hospital in Carson City. She had not been able to get out of bed that morning and had not eaten for a "couple of days," according to the care facility. Feedback from the hospital was not good. Shirley and I headed for Carson City. As we were driving through Sacramento, Barb called to say that Mom had passed away. What a shock that after ailing for only a few days, she just left. At least she did not experience prolonged suffering.

We met Barb the next morning. Mom's body was delivered to the local mortuary, where we made arrangements for her cremation. We then collected her few things from the care facility. It was all pretty straightforward, without much emotion or sorrow. It seems that I said my goodbyes little by little as I visited her and witnessed her decline into a shrinking world. By the time she left, I could freely let her go.

I have forgiven Mom for all the pain she allowed in my life. I was not a victim, but a participant in a difficult childhood that taught me so much and equipped me to handle life as a survivor and succeed. I saw how Mom was a product of her own upbringing by a very domineering and controlling mother in a shaky marriage devoid of much love. I saw how dependent her mother allowed her to become and how she sought the love and support from any man who just might provide it.

I remain ever grateful to her for the devoted care she gave me when I was bedridden those two years. I only regret that we were never able to discuss what we were both experiencing during those early years that included my father's departure, her many men, the suicide, dynamics with her mother, her care for me after my motorcycle crash, and so much more.

Mom.

Chapter 13

An Upward Career Trajectory

The Phone Company—Sacramento

I held several jobs while working for the phone company in Sacramento. They included working in the statistician's office, the plant department budgeting group, and the accounting department, where I managed several first-line supervisors with more than 100 keypunch operators.

In those days, the mid-60's, long distance calls were generally placed with a toll operator who marked essential billing and calling information on a card. These cards from all over northern California were delivered to my section where the information was manually typed into a keypunch machine. The key-punched cards were then fed into huge, tape-driven IBM computers which read the holes in the cards and computed billing information that ended up in customers' phone bills. It was all quite labor intensive. The IBM computers occupied a huge, air-conditioned room on a raised floor with many tape drives, computer cabinets, and huge printers. The job was pretty boring, except for handling two transgender people and dealing with bathroom usage and dress code adjustments—yes, the phone company had a dress code then.

I was transferred to the plant service center serving south Sacramento. Reporting to me were six supervisors who managed repair service clerks who took trouble calls from: customers; deskmen who tested phone lines for repairmen; and line assigners who kept records identifying all the connections of each customer's pair of phone wires. This job was more interesting, having to coordinate with the outside repair staff and handle the ever-changing workload caused by storms, power outages, hungry squirrels eating cables, etcetera.

By now I was approaching 10 years of employment with the phone company. It became clear that I probably would not reach district level management—the next level above my second level. But what haunted me most was that while working for this huge company, I had very little influence on my career path and felt I made no real impact. If I quit going to work, no one would even notice I was gone! I realized that I needed to equip myself with skills that would give me career options and allow me to take some control over my future.

I decided to pursue an MBA by taking evening classes at Sacramento State College. I think I completed two classes and realized that getting an MBA would not readily help me achieve the career control I wanted. But, I thought that becoming a lawyer sure could!

No Victims

While working for the phone company, I often encountered other employees who hated what they were doing, or wanted to do something else, but felt trapped. They'd say they had all their years of service and couldn't give up the retirement and pension benefits in order to pursue their dreams. In their own minds, they were victims, trapped. Many were bitter or depressed about it. They lived for weekends!

Perhaps because of the values I'd developed and what I was learning from our involvement with "consciousness raising" activities and groups, I saw this kind of thinking as crazy—like a self-inflicted prison. I saw no victims. We all have choices and alternatives, but we may not want to take the chance or pay the price of pursuing an alternative. But not deciding is the same as actually choosing to stay where you are. When we consciously understand this choice, we are free. We see that we've chosen to be where we are because we don't like the price that change would mean. That's okay. We're not in a lousy situation because something or someone forced us, but we have chosen to be, consciously or not.

Consciousness Raising

Shirley and I both sought growth: personal, emotional, and spiritual. Our early years together coincided with the so-called "consciousness raising movement," which aimed to help people find deeper meaning and fulfillment in their lives. A really popular movement at the time was EST, whose goal was to release the past to create a more satisfying existence. We participated in the Creative Initiative Foundation (CIF) and soon led groups. It was about seeing reality, understanding cause and effect in our lives, and learning the freedom we all have to make conscious choices. Taking time to look critically at what shapes our thinking and our situations, and seeing alternatives, was very enriching. I also saw that most of our frustrations and problems resulted from wrong or poorly conditioned thinking. That thinking can be changed for the better.

Another growth experience we enjoyed while living in Mill Valley was called STAR (I forgot what the letters stand for). We learned how much past "conditioning" affects our lives. It included sessions where I could express previously unexpressed anger associated with a past experience. Meditation was also an important part of STAR. These experiences provided a grounded sense of who I was, a more conscious awareness of the choices I could make, and the influence my thinking had on the quality of my life and my relationships. In a word, Shirley and I have been "seekers."

Law School

A well-respected, evening law school had been operating in Sacramento for many years. McGeorge School of Law was an independent law school catering to working professionals. Its three-year, evening curriculum included summers. I thought that this would definitely give me the career control I sought. Shirley reluctantly supported me. Little did we know at the outset just what a price this would require of us and our daughters. I've wondered whether I would have pursued this had I known the cost.

Classes were three nights each week. I would leave work and head for law school, getting home around 9:30 p.m., studying until midnight, rising at 6:30 a.m., and starting another day. Saturday was study group, where two other students and I analyzed the cases we studied. We remained a group for the entire three years and relied on each other to get through the required intellectual rigor.

The demanding routine felt like living in a tunnel. The only free time was half of Sunday. The toll on our family was huge. I just wasn't there as a husband or father. I remember one Saturday afternoon while studying, Michelle came into my study asking if

I could play with her—I just sat on the floor hugging her, crying with shame and sorrow for what we were both missing, but mostly what I was taking from her.

The discipline and focus law school required while working and trying to be a husband and father was immense. I was not a stellar student. It was really difficult. The toughest class was Constitutional Law taught by the recently retired US Supreme Court Justice Anthony Kennedy! That's my claim to legal fame! I think I got a C-minus.

Graduation was a proud day for me but, it did not bring completion. I still had to pass the bar exam. I soon took an exhaustive bar exam preparatory course. The bar exam itself was two-and-a-half grueling days. The results are not available for about three months. I'll never forget driving up the hill to our house in Tam Valley with the family and opening the mail box on the road to find the envelope from the State Bar. Trembling, I opened it and saw that I had passed! We all yelled, hugged, and jumped up and down. What a relief. It had remained unsaid—but understood—that if I hadn't passed, I would lose my job on the phone company's legal staff in San Francisco. The stakes were high!

Practicing Law

My original plan was to go into private practice. As I approached graduation, having spent 10 years with the phone company and with a family to support, I began to think about lobbying to join my employer's legal department in San Francisco. I just chickened out of going on my own. I secured important references, had interviews, and was finally offered a position on what was a small legal staff at headquarters in SF.

We bought a nice house in Tam Valley, next to Mill Valley, as it offered a relatively short commute (one hour each way) and was a beautiful place. The kids attended the local Waldorf School in Mill Valley. Shirley set about helping a woman carpenter finish a ground floor room and did some pottery.

I remember clearly those first few days, commuting on the bus over the Golden Gate Bridge. The view of the ocean and city was incredible, yet I noticed that everyone else on the bus focused all their attention on the morning newspaper! I was appalled. But, guess what I was doing after a few days on the bus? Ignoring the view and reading the paper! It was a good demonstration of how easy it is to take beauty, health, and blessings for granted and get mesmerized by routine.

Practicing law was not how I had envisioned it would be. I practiced "regulatory law." It's hard not to yawn when saying that! It was very boring and when I dealt with attorneys on the other side, it was quite stressful. I practiced before administrative law judges of the public utilities commission. It did not require much legal creativity or strategy, and the rules of evidence were very relaxed. But, I did have a nice view of SF Bay from my 14th floor office window where my mind sailed too often. The idea of losing more than two hours each day while commuting to a dreary job began to feel wrong; this was not what life should be about.

I have a choice… No victims!!

Another epiphany: In the midst of this malaise, one day it struck me that here I was at age 35, and I could see the rest of my life! When I was 65, I would be practicing regulatory law with the phone company, commuting from and living in Tam Valley with a boat in Sausalito, waiting to retire.

Oh, no!! I felt like I was suffocating. Then one day, over brown bag lunches in Union Square, a colleague shared that he had received a letter from a school acquaintance: the cable TV company that employed him needed to hire an in-house attorney. My colleague was not interested. I told him that I was, and asked him for the letter.

Cable TV

After learning what cable television was, but still unable to answer why anyone would pay to watch TV, Shirley and I flew to Eugene, Oregon, to interview with Liberty Communications, a cable TV company with several small systems in the midwest and south. They also owned the local Eugene network TV station. I was interviewing for their in-house legal counsel position. The president and I hit it off, but the job was about more regulatory law, which we agreed probably wasn't the right fit for me. So, we departed.

About a month later, the president, Don Tykeson, called me to say that the regional manager of their five midwest cable systems had suddenly died. They needed to replace him. He asked if I'd be interested, since my management and regulatory legal experience was a good fit.

"I may be," I said, having absolutely no clue about the future of this business. It simply provided a change, an adventure, something new.

Our family decided that Michelle and I should go to Adrian, Michigan, where we would live, and look around. Our votes would determine whether I'd take the job and we'd all move. It was May. When we woke up in the Holiday Inn and looked out the window, we saw new snow on the ground! It was beautiful, and that's likely what tipped the scale in favor of the job and this place. It would be an adventure. I called Shirley to let her know. She remembers lounging in the warm sun on our deck in Tam Valley hearing about snow in Michigan!

Our family adventure began as we loaded our VW camper van with baskets of plants, our Labrador dog, two kids, and stuff for the trip to Michigan by way of Yellowstone Park. Now, Adrian is a small, farm-oriented town that progress had left behind. As we arrived and drove around, we could have been aliens from Mars by the looks people gave us. This was 1976, when California and hippies were synonymous. So that became our local identity!

We bought a house built in 1904 in the historic district. Maintenance was a challenge, but it was gracious and spacious. Adrian turned out to be pleasant enough, but adjusting might have been easier if we had moved to a foreign country. Customs, values, and "how we do it here" were alien to us. Shirley attended some college art classes and volunteered at the Crisis Hotline. Michelle and Lisa overcame the challenges of being transplants at grammar and middle school.

I enjoyed managing the cable systems that served small towns in Michigan and Indiana. I had to travel some, especially when attempting to win a franchise to build a system in Burlington, Iowa. The satisfaction of growing the systems, meeting budgets, and working with front-line staff was rewarding. I also thrived on my own while my boss was many miles and states away in Eugene.

Chapter 14

Finding My Father

Exploring My Ancestry

That my paternal grandparents immigrated from Czechoslovakia through Ellis Island and, as a coal miner, my grandfather put three sons through college, had always captivated me. I thought about their courage, discipline, trust, and hard work. What were their values and culture like? I had to know more about my heritage.

My father left us when I was six. Zero contact with him had occurred since then. The only connection in the early years of his departure was from his older brother, Monsignor John Stim, who kindly sent money to my mother to help with our needs.

I wasn't aware of any resentment that my father had left. I really didn't feel that any connection ever existed with him. But, between the nagging need to learn more of my heritage, and to simply close what felt like an open chapter that my father left in my life, I decided it was time to find him.

In 1978, I was traveling through O'Hare Airport in Chicago and noticed a large circle of phone books from around the country. This was long before the Internet and this seemed a good place to search. I was surprised that staring at me from this multitude of books was one from New Jersey. I recalled that my Uncle John had been in New Jersey. Newark didn't seem right, but Passaic felt right. I found a Monsignor Stim! My heart was racing, because this had to be him, and finding him meant that I had to take the next step.

When I arrived home in Adrian, I collected the courage to call him. He answered! I told him who I was, and he remembered, asking how my Mother and sister were. I told him I wanted to contact my father and hoped he could help. He said my father lived in Joplin, Missouri, and provided his phone number.

Boy, this is getting real now!!

In a few days, after rehearsing what I might say to my father, I called. He answered! I told him I was his son, Mike, by his ex-wife, Lillian. He said he had no son named Mike. I was not backing down now! I told him more about me. He didn't hang up, but began to tell me why he left—that my grandmother was difficult and so on. The conversation was quite rambling. He said he was managing the oldest bar west of the Mississippi. I told him I would like to visit him to learn more about my grandparents and what he knew of their lives and histories. He said okay. I said I would call him soon to pick a date to do so.

Wow! This is really going to happen. I felt like I might have opened Pandora's box or was sliding down the rabbit hole as I plunged into this scary chapter of discovery. The trip and visit with Alex was terrifying, revealing, and rewarding—times ten!! I wrote about the experience as it happened. Though lengthy, the following passage explains how it all unfolded:

8/12/78 9:45 a.m.

I am driving and within 50 miles of where I'll meet my father. I can't believe it—I've had so many feelings and anticipations about this moment, yet, it's as though once I decided to do it, crossed over, then the way seemed to part before me.

*I feel solid—very good physically and grounded and in touch emotionally. I feel **very** excited and without expectations. This is what living is about—it is such a beautiful adventure. The world looks so beautiful. I don't see a hostile element in it. How beautiful and filling it is to be free—to open to what's around me now and whatever is in the future. I want to hang on to this, yet I know that is the very trap I'm generally in with my life: "hang on tight, be in control, know the outcome, and change all I can to maintain control and **create** the outcome." How limiting, how deathly, how impossible!*

When meditating last night, I saw and embraced my father's true self. He was beautiful, strong, warm, supportive, and loving. Let me see that true self in him today. Let me feel this experience to the fullest. Let me "see" myself. Let my eyes be opened to see and love the more of me that I'll be exposed to today: my strengths, weaknesses (34 miles—Oh, God!), my origins, my dark side and light side, and the part of him that is me.

What will it be like? What does he look like? Where do we look similar? What does he like or dislike to do, eat, experience? What has he done these past 30 years? Has he ever thought much about me or Mom? Ever feel guilty? How does he feel about himself? Does he have friends? What kind? What was his childhood like, his brothers, parents? Geez, I'm scared!

Don't let me get away from this by skipping on the surface. But, don't let it hurt a lot either! Oh, hell—let it hurt! (28 miles now!) It can't be any worse than the pains and hurts of the past 30 years, and that, with much growth. The unknown is so exciting. I know I'll be different. This will affect me in so many ways. Let it happen! My task and commitment is to be open, to let it in, to experience, to be where I am with what and who I am. Nothing else in the world matters right now but this. This is as total an experience as I've ever had. (24 miles) I love life for that too, damn it!

I had no trouble finding the bar. What a let-down when I saw that dump. A corner bar without a name sign outside, just some beer signs. It was in an old decrepit building needing paint and life. So much for the "oldest bar west of the Mississippi!" I did not want to go inside. I wanted to run. Then I hoped this really wasn't the right place. But, it was and I did what I came to do—I walked in, opening an old, rusty, creaky screen door and smelling sour beer. The door slammed shut behind me, announcing my arrival.

It was dim and dingy inside. I looked expectantly. At 11:30 a.m., seven or eight unkempt old guys (aka: bar flies) were sitting at the bar, hunched over their drinks. They turned to look at me with expectant grins. My father shuffled around the end of the bar. He was short and dark-complected with a couple days of whiskers. His clothes were well-worn and drab. His two front teeth were missing! God, this can't be him. But, of course it is, stupid. This is your father! He shook my hand, half smiling as he mustered all the emotion he could allow himself.

In that moment, what my senses saw didn't matter. Here was my very own father. It was like searching for and finding a long lost treasure that the coarser elements of life and time had permanently disfigured. But, that didn't change the fact that here is that treasure—it exists for me.

My father introduced me to the old cronies at the bar. They expressed all the good feelings they knew. The bar was the sleaziest I have ever been in. I sat at the bar across from my father. I had one beer. I met the few patrons who came in. It wasn't easy to talk to my father. What was there to say? We did the small talk. In about half an hour, his wife, Terry, came in to relieve him. She was very pleasant, hefty, and about 50 years old. I liked her.

My father was sober. He said he hadn't had a drink for two months. I believed him. He said he had quite a drinking problem and began to have health problems, so he quit. He just isn't as I'd pictured him to be these many years. He's older-looking, not fat, but his skin sags and seems completely lifeless. But, there was an intensity and spark in his eyes at times that sadly expressed how he betrayed his true self all his life. I see myself there—I could have been him—I am capable of being there, too.

We drove to his rented house they've had for two years. He owns another house that they don't live in, but I'll get to that later. He has five kids: Mark is 19, a good looking, physically active fellow. Joel is 18, a confused boy on the effeminate side. He's easy to talk to and very sensitive. He doesn't know what he wants to do. He's the disappointment to his Dad, who doesn't understand him. Tammy is 15, a beautiful girl who is quiet and withdrawn. She's very athletic and plays on boys' hardball teams, for which her Dad is very proud.

Michelle (Shelly) is 11. She's also very pretty. She has a sparkle and innocence that I hope she doesn't lose. Kris is four. She is a darling, very smart little girl. And, she's spoiled rotten as "the apple of my eye" as her Dad puts it. Her sisters wait on her and keep her occupied. It's as though Dad is spoiling her as he was spoiled, being the youngest in his family.

Tammy told me, in response to my questioning, that Alex got very grouchy and mean when he was drinking and that he was drinking a lot. I suspect that was when he got physically violent with Mom and me 30 years earlier. Ironically, Alex told me Mom's mother (Baba) had slapped him once. I wonder what that was about?

The rented house they lived in is old, in the older part of town. The inside floors and walls were dirty. The place was poorly kept. The furniture looked to be second-hand and in disrepair. The main bathroom sink was plugged, a light was out in the other bathroom, and one TV stacked upon two others worked with half a picture on the screen. There were numerous unfinished projects strewn around. The whole scene would take all the enthusiasm and motivation out of anyone living there. It's like: "What's the use?" Yet, no one thing, by itself, was a major project to get in order.

Alex, Kris, and I went to Sambo's (like a Denny's) for lunch. Here I saw Alex ignore Kris and what she was saying. As Kris kept talking and pestering for attention, the more resolved he was to ignore her. When I looked at her and held her hand and told her to be quiet for a minute, that she would be next, she was quiet—for a short while. I saw Alex get up and go after the waitress for something she forgot. So, he does act. But, was that just a show for me?

Then came the most unbelievable part of the visit. We went to the house they own to feed the animals: two geese, six ducks, and two dogs—St. Bernards! Alex warned me that it was a mess outside and inside and that he wouldn't let me see inside. After being in their rented house,

I thought I had prepared myself well. The house was a ranch style on a big lot on the outskirts of town in a decent area. The house looked sound from the outside, but the yard was an overgrown mess. Trash is piled up against the garage door. The animals live in a messy, makeshift pen. ("Makeshift" seems the word for his life and I'd add irresponsible, slovenly, lazy, irrational, blaming, don't give a damn.)

I asked if I could help carry a large bag of feed he was carrying to the house. He said I could hold the front door, then said to come on in. God, I have never, ever been in anything as revolting in my life. The smell overwhelmed me. I was surrounded by piles of rotten food, urine, mold, dog crap, garbage, and trash. There were empty bags of dog food, half empty cartons of ice cream, cans, bottles. If it belonged in a landfill, it was piled there in their house!

I honestly don't believe the house was salvageable. I was so repulsed, I couldn't believe what I saw. "This can't be," I told myself. How could he have let this happen? NO, how could HE have done this? It is animal, inhuman. He made light of it by saying, "Didn't I tell you it was a mess?" I find it difficult to think of this part of my experience, even now. It's just impossible to understand it. How can it be? What must he think of himself to live like this or his family who lived it, too. Even the poorest Mexican shacks I've seen can't compare. Just imagine, their own garbage and filth drove them out of the house they owned to a rental! Instead of cleaning their own mess, they paid rent to someone else. I was sick and wanted to leave for home right then. No, I would stick it out 'til morning, then I could leave forever. I would remain as immersed as I can be for this time. It is what I came for, but I was not looking forward to spending the night at their rented house.

We finally left this dump and went to another dump: the bar. Apparently Alex spends time there, even though there is a bartender on duty. He thinks that fraternizing with the customers is good for business. We played shuffleboard and I met more of the old, broken-down cronies. They were all as pleasant as their half-toothless selves could be. I don't mean to sound so judgmental. I'm just not used to such company.

We then went to their rented house. I had a nice chat with Terri and with Tammy and Michelle. We spent much time sitting in front of the half-picture, black and white TV, sitting on broken-down furniture. Alex fixed a surprisingly good dinner: ham, peas, beans, salad, radishes, and pickles. After dinner, we went back to the bar. I had two beers; Alex had Coke. We played more shuffleboard. The smoke really hurt my eyes and I was relieved to leave about 10:30. The room I slept in had clean sheets and was all tidied up. I said goodnight at 12, leaving Alex and Mark in front of the TV. The girls were playing in their room. I was very tired and glad to be leaving the next morning.

I arose at 7:30 a.m., washed, and shaved. Alex was sitting in the TV room. I said I'd be leaving soon. He suggested we go to Denny's for breakfast, as it was near the freeway. I thought that was a great idea. Everyone but Michelle was still sleeping. I said goodbye to her and we left.

We had a pretty good talk over breakfast. It started when I said how good I thought the visit had been. He agreed, saying he sure didn't know what to expect. I then asked him about his parents and childhood, as this was my real reason for the visit. He was the youngest of two brothers; about six years younger than John. He said he was his Mom's favorite, which made his brothers jealous. His father was shorter than him; Alex is 5'8"—same as me.

My grandfather came to America when he was about 30. He and my grandmother came with a number of other related families to Nesquehoning, PA. He was a coal miner and he drank a lot. Alex said he thought it helped him live longer by washing down the coal dust. He had a copper still and made booze for his own consumption. My grandmother never learned to speak English. The Slavs stuck together and spoke only Slavic. Alex said he wondered how he made it through grammar school, as he spoke no English at home! Alex made very few visits to his parents once an adult. There were no other family ties in the U.S. except an aunt and cousin near Nesquehoning.

Alex's father was very strict. It was unusual if he didn't use his strap on Alex twice in a week. He told of a time when, in the tenth grade, he got home one hour later than he promised. When his dad got the strap out and was about to let him have it, Alex hugged his dad, pinning his arms down and said, "Dad, I'm too old for that now, I didn't do anything wrong by being a little late—now don't hit me anymore." His dad told him to leave. He left for a few days and returned when tensions had eased.

Here's a recipe of his mom's which he still makes: Potato pancakes. Take six potatoes, peel and grate finely and drain the liquid well. Add two eggs and mix with about 3/4 cups flour to make a fairly dry mixture. Bring about 3/4" of oil to near-boil in a skillet. Spoon out a large lump with a tablespoon, smash into the pan about 3/8" thick. Cook till golden brown and crisp. Drain on paper towel. They're good cold, too — Alex used to eat these as a kid.

He told me how he worked at the local A&P market doing odd jobs after school. The boss once asked him how he could get rid of a load of bread. Alex said he'd go door-to-door with loaves on his wagon. They bought the idea and that started a door-to-door sales effort that was very successful for him.

Alex really came alive when he told me of the innovative and successful marketing ideas he had at various stores where he worked, like giving a pair of nylon pantyhose away with the purchase of a woman's suit, which weren't selling well. Pantyhose were scarce at the time. And, how he'd sell pantyhose by putting his fist in and showing how sheer they were.

After Alex married mom, he worked for my grandmother and grandfather. He started at their Silverton, Oregon store. He did not get along with my grandmother. I doubt any son-in-law could. But he respected her business sense. He liked my grandfather, who he said was a great mens' clothing salesman. He thinks their relationship started downhill when they bought the West Portal store in San Francisco, which was all children's clothes. This was my grandmother's thing. Grandfather was out of his element. It is during this period that they divorced. Alex changed jobs often, but it was always in merchandising.

It was time for me to say goodbye and head home. I was satisfied and proud. I learned more about my heritage and faced my past. It was revealing that during the entire visit and my many questions, Alex never asked a single question of me or my family! We said our goodbyes, promising to keep in touch. But, I knew, even then, that it would not happen. It didn't have to!!

Reflections on the way home from a very long journey: I've been on the way to myself! There are no other voices now but mine. Other voices may arise, voices of my father or others, but mine will be loudest, and I will listen. I feel a deep calm and assurance. I am very proud and happy to be me. I must be the most fortunate person alive. I am so grateful not to have lived with my father any more than I did during childhood. This is a huge revelation: to be grateful he left! I feel a deep love and gratitude for my mother, despite all her shortcomings. I am so proud and thankful that I have the courage to do what I've done and for the vision to see and be driven to do what I must for truth in my life, no matter what the pain. No, there is no reason now to be in touch with my father again. It's finished. The circle has been closed... with gratitude.

Chapter 15

Enter Christian Science

Spiritual Seekers Find a Home

Shirley and I had not been particularly "religious," although we tended more toward thoughts "spiritual" in regards to the Divine. The values we picked up through our earlier consciousness work opened us to spirituality. We had been members of the Presbyterian Church in Sacramento. I had even been a Deacon. When we moved to a different church, the minister visited us with some questions. When he learned that we both believed we could pray directly to God instead of "through" Jesus, he suggested we'd be more comfortable elsewhere! That was a shocker to us. When we moved to Tam Valley, we tried the Unitarian Church and felt much more at home with our beliefs.

While in Adrian, Shirley had painful back problems. She got some relief from a local chiropractor. The pain got severe one morning and she found that her chiropractor was away on vacation. A neighbor friend who was a Christian Scientist suggested she call a particular Christian Science Practitioner for help. She called her, and within an hour was completely free of the pain. The Practitioner, a dear Mrs. Curtis, in answer to Shirley's inquiry, told her when she did her prayerful work and it was exactly when Shirley received relief. This was the beginning of our study of Christian Science and the incredible blessings it brought in the form of physical healings, improved relationships, solving life challenges, and more. We had no idea then just how much we would be relying on it over the next year and a half. Indeed, it became an important part of our lives through today, 40 years later!

Through The Rain

We were in Adrian for two years when I was asked to move to Portland to build and operate the cable system on the west side and compete to win the franchise for the east side. Little did I know that this would precipitate the most trying and painful period of our marriage and family experience. I decided to take the new position, since I had done all I believed I could do where I was. But, I gave no heed to Shirley's objections to leaving Adrian. She had adjusted, found friends, and was enjoying her art and volunteer work. She felt that I just ran over her on my way to Portland. She was right.

The Portland job was very challenging. I undertook a heavy load: building the new system; locating, building out, and staffing a large office; doing the political work; and preparing our franchise proposal to build the east side. I think the biggest problem for me was that my boss, the president, grew up in Portland and leaned over my shoulder too much of the time.

Our family didn't adjust to Portland well. School and friends were not very positive for the girls, and Shirley never connected. We decided we needed to make a change. The idea that appealed was to buy a small business we could devote ourselves to in a location we liked.

Santa Cruz seemed a good choice. We used a business broker who recommended two businesses located beside each other. One was a fast food hot dog restaurant. The other—a coffee bean and tea shop. I did virtually no due diligence to evaluate the businesses, except to review the financials supplied to us. We used all our savings as a down payment to buy them, along with a note to the sellers for the balance.

I gave my boss notice that I would be resigning in 30 days. He was very disappointed. Shirley and the girls moved in with her parents in Capitola so she could begin running the businesses, awaiting my arrival. Within two weeks, it became clear that the revenue from the businesses, especially the coffee store, were insufficient to support us. It looked like the financial records had been falsified. They overstated the actual revenue because, as we later learned, the seller took a large share of the business with him. So, we had invested all of our savings and taken on a large debt in businesses that could not support us.

As we have done with many of our challenges, we called Mrs. Curtis for spiritual help. She asked to talk with me and told me very directly: "You get that job back!" Retracting my resignation was one of the most difficult things I'd ever done. It was humiliating. I was not told that my retraction was accepted, but I kept going to work, doing my job, and getting paid. Within a few months, a man was hired to "help" me manage the job. It was soon clear that he would be my replacement. My days were numbered!

I would fly to San Jose every other weekend to be with Shirley and the kids, who stayed with her parents in Capitola during this time. They were so generous and gracious in their help. That was the most painful period for all of us and it lasted ONE WHOLE

YEAR until we unwound our mess. Shirley had very debilitating back problems, but she kept opening and running the coffee shop with help while she would lay down on a mattress in the back room, simultaneously working with Mrs. Curtis and studying Christian Science. It went on for months. Don't know how she did it.

We went to a local lawyer in Santa Cruz. I picked him from a lawyers' reference guide because he appeared well connected. When we told him the story of our mess, he said to me: "As a lawyer, how could you possibly have done something so stupid?" It didn't help that he was arrogant and pompous, but what he said was exactly right—how could I have created this terrible situation and cause my family such suffering!? When we left his office, I sat in the car sobbing with deep humiliation and guilt.

We pressed on with a lawsuit against the seller of the coffee store. Shirley went to the deposition and a pre-trial conference, which our lawyer said she didn't have to attend. At the conference, the judge asked her questions directly. At the conclusion, he told the seller's lawyer he would lose and had better settle. We did settle by giving the business back to the seller in exchange for canceling the large debt we owed him. We also sold the fast food hot dog restaurant for what we owed.

Finally, we had put this terrible mess behind us. We had lost our savings, but we were together at our home in Portland at last. It was so incredibly joyful. I grew to appreciate family like never before.

The next challenge was to find a new job, knowing that the number of days left on my current job were shrinking as my replacement had all but taken over. I had help from Mrs. Curtis and was praying to get a clear understanding of employment and supply. I came to see clearly that a job is about supply, but fulfillment was a spiritual quality unrelated to what we do for a paycheck. This understanding is what I bring with me to a job, to relationships with family and friends, and while exercising or eating or doing anything else in life.

I put my resume out and got a call to interview for a regional manager position with Comcast. Shirley and I traveled to their headquarters in Philadelphia and interviewed with the founder, Ralph Roberts (father of Brian, the current CEO) and two others. Nothing felt right about it.

Then, a few days later, I received a call from a man I had met by phone while in Adrian regarding something about the Michigan Cable TV Association that I belonged to then. Tim Neher worked for Continental Cablevision in Michigan and was being promoted to executive vice president in Boston. He had to find his replacement and had heard good things about me and thought we should meet if I were interested. Wow, was I!

We met for an interview at O'Hare Airport in Chicago. I learned that the job would be in Michigan, with an office in Lansing, and I'd be responsible for several cable systems there and for franchising new communities. The pay was reasonable, but the stock plan was very generous. They would cover moving expenses, too. Although it seemed weird that we'd be going back to Michigan, this was a truly amazing demonstration of the power of prayer. I felt lifted from a limb being sawed off to a place of harmony, light, and strength. There is no way to explain this as simply coincidence. The timing of this perfect opportunity was a demonstration of the Divine in action. This opportunity was this single biggest blessing in my life in terms of employment, supply, success, and ethical values. More on this amazing experience later.

I later wondered how I came to be considered for this position, since I did not have a wide-ranging reputation in the cable industry. Then I realized that I had participated in a "road show" with Liberty Communications when they made an attempt at going public. I presented the operations side of the company to potential investment bankers. One of the presentations was in Boston, where the two founders of Continental Cablevision attended. They may have remembered me.

Also, when attempting to win a franchise for Liberty in Fondulac, Wisconsin, my boss, Don Tykeson, hired Rex Bradley as a consultant to help me. Rex had been president of a cable television company and of the National Cable Television Association. We spent time together and hit it off very well. He knew those two Continental founders well and may have put in a good word for me. Nevertheless, that Tim would call me about this position that changed the rest of our lives when I had just a few days left in my job with Liberty was more than miraculous.

My departure from Liberty was harmonious. The one thing I remember that Don Tykeson said to me was, "Don't sell your Liberty stock." I had received a few non-public shares while with the company. That turned out to be good advice. The future proceeds from the sale of that stock made possible the purchase of our first sailboat. We named it "Liberty."

Lessons From Going Through "The Rain"

1. We cannot know in advance the good that our best work, ethic, and reputation can do for us. It should be enough for us to know that it matters in many ways, even if we don't witness the effect.
2. Human willfulness leads to suffering. That suffering, if acute enough, will ultimately turn us to divine help and teach us to listen and follow higher guidance. Until that happens, suffering continues!
3. A job is not about "fulfillment," it is about supply for our physical needs. Fulfillment comes from our spiritual, emotional, and interpersonal progress. We bring that progress with us in all endeavors, including the job, which in turn, can improve the employment experience and all other situations.
4. There are no victims. This is a vital lesson. We all have choices. Even the belief that one is "locked in" to an unpleasant situation is a choice. We just don't like the alternatives enough to change our situation, so staying put *is* the choice one makes. Hence, there is no blame. That is very freeing.

Section 6

Continental Cablevision & Sailing

Chapter 16

Moving Back to Michigan

A Winning Move

After leaving Michigan for Portland, we never dreamed we'd ever return. Yet, we were on our way back! The girls thought it was okay, as their memories of Adrian were good, and Lansing was far closer to our comfort level, especially with East Lansing being the home of Michigan State University and Lansing the state capital, and a job that had much promise for me.

Michelle said it would work for her if we bought a riding lawn-mower she could use. Lisa's deal was to have a horse. We bought a house surrounded by a huge lawn and Michelle was happy to ride the mower a few times (Dad did the rest!). We were able to lease a horse at a small stable located just a bike ride from our house. Lisa's job was to regularly clean the stall and exercise the horse. She did dressage with it for a time. After two years or so, her interests changed, so we gave up the lease; much easier than trying to sell a horse!

We were active in the local Christian Science church, played couples tennis and even some bridge. It was a comfortable life, and although I spent many late evenings working, I rarely worked on weekends, although the boat we had at Holland, Michigan took me away from family time too often to suit Shirley.

Lisa, Shirley, Michelle & Mike in Michigan (1981)

Continental was headquartered in Boston. It operated with a decentralized management style. Its management philosophy was to hire high quality regional managers who had all the authority and resources they needed to manage and grow their part of the company. The only serious oversight came once a year when I would submit a detailed capital and operating budget for the following year. If I met the budget during the year, I rarely heard from Boston. It was classic decentralized management and unique in the industry. I thrived in this environment. I loved the job and the values of its key people.

I was vice president and regional manager for Michigan, which initially included our systems in Lansing, Jackson, Roseville, and Madison Heights. Besides managing these systems with 100-plus employees, my task was to win franchises and build new cable systems. The Detroit suburbs were actively inviting proposals from interested cable companies. This was time-consuming and involved winning over city council members and key constituents and preparing a well-crafted and responsive franchise proposal.

This was very competitive, usually with four to six other cable companies vying for the same franchises. Competition and ambitions caused some companies to promise more than they knew they could deliver in order to win. I could not do that and believed the most important qualities to winning were a demonstrated track record of integrity and ethical, responsive operation of our existing cable systems. We won all of the franchises for which we competed. The communities in which we built cable systems were Southfield, Hazel Park, Oak Park, Dearborn Heights, Westland, and Bloomfield Hills. We became the largest cable operator in Michigan at that time.

The financial stakes in this franchising competition were very high. And the ethics of competing companies varied a lot. The heat of this competition led to some questionable outcomes. I'll share the story of one of these.

A Mayor Goes to Prison—Winning Without Being Tainted!

Westland, a suburb of Detroit to the southwest, had issued an RFP (request for proposals) for a cable TV system to serve the community. As was our practice, in preparation for drafting our proposal, we began spending time getting to know the community, key organizations, and city council members. We also hired two local, influential lawyers that were partners. I offered a modest bonus to the lawyers, should we be successful.

Then I got a call from the president of Cox Cable in Atlanta, against whom we often competed. He told me that he had received a call from an FBI agent who asked to meet him on a street corner. When he did, the agent asked him to wear a wire to record a talk with the mayor of Westland during a golf game with him. He declined, deciding that he would not pursue this franchise, given the possible mess and negative press, as Cox was a publicly traded company. He was kind enough to call me with this "heads up" warning for which I was extremely grateful. I decided that being forewarned, we would pursue the franchise with all the caution and propriety possible.

One day as we were busy preparing our proposal, I received an urgent call from our lawyers asking to meet for lunch that day. At our lunch meeting, they told me that they could assure me of winning the franchise, but they needed triple the bonus I had promised. They implored me to do this. This smelled very bad.

"No way," I said. "We will win this on the merits, if at all."

The mayor had hand-picked a "Cable Commission" who were charged with reviewing the proposals received and recommending the winner to the mayor and city council. Fortunately, they hired an independent consultant to review and rank the proposals. The consultant was knowledgeable and professional. He ranked the five proposals received, recommending Continental's as the best. The Cable Commission met, reviewed the consultants' recommendations, and unanimously decided to recommend the lowest-ranked company, Storer Communications, to the mayor and council as the company that should receive the franchise! It was clear that "the fix was in."

Very soon thereafter, word was out that the mayor had been indicted by the grand jury for soliciting bribes. It was all over the newspapers. The city council had no choice but to disregard the recommendation of the mayor's very tainted Cable Commission, and rely on the only objective and untainted input available—the consultant's recommendation. So, we won the franchise. The mayor went to prison for several years. And, despite the poisoned franchising process, we were never tainted or suspected of wrongdoing, even though we won. I was very grateful for the protection that surrounded us during this entire process.

Leading by Example

It took a staff of several people to research and prepare the various franchise proposals required to be competitive. As we began competing for several at the same time, I needed to hire a politically astute and persuasive writer. I hired George, who had been a newspaper writer and spent time on political campaigns. He was indeed a good writer, even if a bit too shrewd.

Kathleen was a long-time, well-respected employee that I had assigned to the franchising group well before hiring George. She reported to George, did research, and handled the mechanics of preparing our franchise proposal packages and presentations. A number of glitches began to occur; George blamed Kathleen. Since George was her boss and I held him accountable, I had to support him by allowing him to fire her. Within days of her firing, I began to learn that the problems had been caused by George. This was confirmed as I dug into the situation. Several people close to the situation had known the facts.

It was clear what I needed to do. It was very difficult, but it was the right thing. I fired George. Then I called Kathleen at home to apologize and offer her job back. She accepted. Employees who were aware of what happened praised my decision. I became an instant hero! This underscored for me the importance of ethical leadership in setting the right values of an organization. It does "trickle down."

"I Want Your Job!"

East Lansing is home to Michigan State University. Through a professor acquaintance, I was offered the opportunity to teach an upper division undergraduate class about cable television. It was a wonderful opportunity to connect with bright young people, while sharing some insights on leadership and something about the "real world" of business. The assignment for the semester was for each student to prepare a competitive proposal to a fictional community for a franchise to build a cable TV system; they were required to make an oral presentation to the fictional city council that would convince them theirs was the best proposal for their community.

This was quite a bit of work for a three-unit class. Most students waited toward the end of the semester to really get their proposals together. I was surprised at how poorly written many of them were. Content was fair, but grammar, syntax, and organization was disappointing.

During a general Q&A session, a student asked, "I want your job. How do I get it?" Lots of heads were nodding at that. It was clear that they wanted to learn the fast track to success! I shared with them that success required the important qualities of: a strong work ethic; integrity; and experience based on learning by actually doing the basics. And, although having a goal is helpful, success is a byproduct of how one has excelled at whatever the task is at the time. Shortcuts do not exist. The most important job is not the one you are ultimately seeking, but the one you have now.

Go Sailing to Get Promoted!

My experience with Continental in Michigan was the most fulfilling work in my life. The Michigan staff grew from about 50 to more than 250 and we quadrupled our number of cable customers. I had great respect for the talented team of people there. We worked hard, valued our customers and employees, and shared an ethic of honesty and responsiveness. Beyond that, the corporate staff in Boston were very bright and ethical people. Most of the senior people had Harvard MBAs. They were smart type A's. The best part of the job was being left alone to do my job and call upon the corporate staff only when I needed specific support, such as in marketing or programming.

Having done the job in Michigan for seven years, I had helped grow our presence in the state as far as it could reasonably grow. Things were good, all of the systems had been built out, and the management staff was strong. It was time to follow a dream: go sailing. This was not a snap decision. In fact, I had told my boss 18 months in advance of when I planned to depart, as I wanted to be sure the transition from my leaving was smooth and successful.

Shirley and I had a plan: go sailing for two years, then figure out what to do next, as we didn't have the funds to completely retire. I was 45 when we left. As departure time got closer, the girls were in college, we sold the house, stored or sold our things, and had our sailboat trucked to Florida. From there, we would begin our new adventure. One month before departure, the president called me to Boston. I thought it was to say "goodbye and good luck," but I was wrong. More on this after some words about this passion of sailing.

Chapter 17

Sailing

The Joy of My Life

"Wonders" in my life: the miracle of witnessing the home births of my grandchildren; the harmony of carving on a snowboard; the beauty and quiet of a mountain hike; being surrounded by the abundance of life while scuba diving; the peace of meditation; touching deep feelings while listening to classic jazz; and the sound of a bow wave under sail. Here's the story on this most essential part of my life and joy: sailing.

A Painful Learning Curve. Learning to sail had so many mess-ups, it's a wonder it ever took hold. But, take hold it did, culminating in a 10-year sailing saga that took me over 50,000 sailing miles around most of the world following my retirement from Continental. Sailing was Shirley's idea as were most of the joyful activities of our lives, such as: windsurfing, scuba diving, and snowboarding.

As we looked out on San Francisco Bay while living in Tam Valley during the Arab gas embargo of the early '70's, seeing all those sailboats moving gracefully without burning fuel was enough for Shirl to arrange sailing lessons for us. We learned the basics of sailing on tiny, eight-foot El Toro sailboats, which tipped a lot when you made a mistake. This meant you were then sitting in six inches of water when things didn't go right. From there, we joined a sailing club in Alameda where, after taking more sailing lessons and getting checked out, we could use 22-foot to 26-foot boats for a day or two on the Bay.

So, one weekend we all boarded our 26-foot sailboat that we had for the two days. Things went okay the first day out. The girls loved being on the bow as we plunged over the waves. In fact, we had to tie them onto the bow railing to keep them aboard!

As the day wore on, we decided to anchor for the night. The night was peaceful enough, but when we awoke the next morning, we were shocked to see that we were not where we had anchored! We had dragged our anchor quite a distance and were lucky we didn't go aground or, worse, get overrun by the many ships plying the Bay. Our sailing experience that day got no better. As I hanked (clipped) on the jib, I later found that I put it on upside down because when the wind piped up, the strain on the upside down sail caused it to rip in half. I was beginning to feel very stupid, but had no thought of giving up.

Some time later, we decided to try another sailing adventure. This one was an even worse experience. We chartered a 28-foot sailboat out of Anacortes, Washington. It was a pretty boat in a beautiful area. We were sailing nicely along, approaching a small island where we were going to anchor for lunch. We dropped the sails and I started the engine. It ran for a while, then suddenly stopped. I discovered that the prop had snagged a line we were dragging in the water. This was serious. I immediately dropped the anchor onto a rocky bottom where holding was questionable. We had no choice. I had to jump into that frigid water and try to cut the line off the propellor and shaft before the anchor dragged and we went aground. I did it, but probably got close to having hypothermia.

I started the engine to move to a better spot to anchor when Michelle yelled to me that the floorboards below were floating!! Yes, the boat was sinking! I concluded that when the line wrapped tightly around the prop shaft, the torque loosened the packing gland nut (a big nut sealing the shaft to the transmission), causing water to enter. I tightened it as best I could. It reduced the water flow significantly. But, a lot more water entered when the engine was running and the prop turning.

We had no choice but to head back to the marina, sailing as much as possible to minimize running the engine and taking on more water. The wind was very strong—thankfully from the right direction for sailing. Then we saw what looked like mountains of water leaping into the air ahead of us. It was a major tidal rip. We couldn't avoid it. As we sailed through it, the water swamped the small dinghy we were towing. It became a sea anchor and nearly stopped our progress. Cheers went up when the tow line finally snapped, allowing us to make better speed home to the marina before we took on much more water. That we lost the dinghy was unimportant at that point.

By then we were all wet, cold, and shivering in the cockpit. The poor kids had to pee so badly, all they could do was pee in their soaking pants, which did give them relief and a bit of warmth! We finally made it back to the marina and I notified the charter company of our plight. I was able to stop most of the leak, so we stayed on the boat that night, grateful that we were out of danger, able to shower, put on dry clothes, and dream of heading home the next day. Did I decide to stop sailing after this? Of course not!

A Sailing Partnership

While living in Tam Valley, we met a couple who were interested in sharing ownership of their 30-foot sailboat. It was docked in Sausalito, just a bike ride away from our house! This worked well, as we could learn from them as we sailed together on the Bay while sharing all expenses. The only new mess-up was running out of gas while taking a friend out for a sail. We hailed a passing boater who kindly towed us to our yacht club where I could get gas. Who knew to check the fuel level in advance? Geez.

What is it about sailing that is so addicting, mesmerizing, and wonderful that kept me at it? Simply put: it is the ultimate dream maker. It's magical to feel the power of the wind silently moving a boat over eight knots, hour after hour, with just the sound of the water rushing by and going anywhere in the world that the ocean touches. The freedom is boundless—that's the fitting name of our boat that eventually took us most of the way around the world.

Our Own Boat

Soon after moving to Lansing for Continental, Liberty Communications was bought by another cable company. We received a large check for the stock we owned; it was enough to buy a new sailboat and then some! So, Shirley and I went to the Annapolis Boat Show, the largest sailboat show in the country. We inspected a few, then while looking at some sailing jewelry met a couple who enthusiastically described their new, 45-foot boat built in Taiwan called a Norseman 447. This was much larger than the 36- to 38-foot size I was considering. But, Shirley insisted we check this out—that we should not limit our thinking.

"Liberty."

Lisa, Shirley, and I aboard "Liberty."

We became good friends with this couple, ordered this boat, and took delivery in Racine, Wisconsin about 16 months later. Shirley's Mom and Dad met us there, where the boat was being commissioned. Then, with Lisa and a friend, we sailed across Lake Michigan to our boat's new home in Holland, Michigan.

This boat was beautiful, appropriately named "Liberty." It had two staterooms, two heads (bathrooms with showers), a roomy galley, and a comfortable salon. It had great lines and sailed well, too. Over the next five summers, we sailed much of Lake Michigan and Lake Ontario. The Canadian shore of Lake Ontario was the most magical of all. One dark night, we even saw the Northern Lights while at anchor in the stillness broken only by the occasional call of a loon!

As we became more comfortable handling the many rigors of sailing longer distances, my dreaming went into overdrive. This could be the vehicle to a new adventure. That's when we agreed that taking two years to go sailing would be a wonderful thing that we could do together and experience everything new. So, the planning began, the timetable was set, and the boat was prepared by adding a water maker, SSB shortwave radio, scuba compressor and tanks, many spare parts, etcetera.

Saying Goodbye to Continental (Or So I Thought!)

Back to that call from the president to come to Boston. Having made the decision to go sailing, I told my boss, Tim Neher, that I would be leaving in 18 months. Continental meant so much to me, I wanted to ensure that my departure was smooth with no lapse in leadership. Then, about a month before my scheduled leave, Tim invited me to Boston for a short meeting.

How nice, I thought, *a personal goodbye!*

Here's how the supposed "goodbye and good luck" meeting actually went. I sat down with Chairman and CEO Amos Hostetter and President Tim Neher. (Tim is the one who hired me to replace him in Michigan when he was moved to Boston).

Amos said, "We'd like to offer you the job of executive vice president here in Boston, managing half of Continental's cable systems."

I was stunned!

"Wow, thanks," I said, "but you know I've been planning to leave Continental to go sailing."

"How long do you plan to do this?"

"For two years," I said.

"Well, we can't hold the job open for you for two years," he said.

I assured him that I completely understood, but that fulfilling this plan was very important to Shirley and me. After some discussion, Amos and Tim shared that they could hold the job for seven months and asked if I would take the job then. I was blown away, as this just wasn't any part of our plan.

Yet, the ability to go sailing for seven months and return to the company that I loved and valued was very appealing. I don't remember taking much time to think about this or even to discuss it with Shirley. I just knew this was right, so I told them I'd take the job in seven months. Thankfully, Shirley agreed. It turned out to be a perfect arrangement!

"Casting Off!" — Not as Easy as It Sounds!

To take off sailing for seven months sounds wonderful, but preparation was overwhelming. Sell the house, store what we wanted to keep, sell the rest, assure our girls that all would be well, say goodbye to our many friends, put financial affairs on hold, arrange for trucking the boat to Florida, accumulate all the navigation charts needed, study weather and understand weather charts, learn the Bahamian immigration and customs requirements, plan for provisioning food aboard for extended periods, set up AT&T high seas phone calling via shortwave radio, and more.

Once the boat arrived at the boatyard in Florida, recommissioning it began. This meant stepping (placing) the mast, installing the boom, attaching and adjusting all the standing rigging, running all the lines, putting three sails on, checking out all electronics and refrigeration, then provisioning the boat for several weeks. This job took two weeks before we were really ready to "cast off" for the Bahamas.

We finally got underway one evening to sail through the night, carefully navigating through the swiftly north-setting Gulf Stream while we set a westerly course. This was long before GPS. Existing land-based loran fixes didn't get further than a few miles offshore and available satnav—satellite navigation—gave a fix only every four to eight hours! So, we got proficient at dead reckoning, which means calculating our current position based on the time, speed, and course made good from our previous known position.

As the sun rose, we saw the low-lying Bahamas. The water color quickly changed from a dark, cobalt blue to a transparent, light blue as the depth rose to just eight feet or so. We tied up at the immigration dock at West End—tired, but elated that we had successfully completed this first step of our new adventure. We had sailed to a new country on our own. The adventure was underway!

Sailing through the Bahamas over the next six months was a wonderful experience. Yes, we endured storms, fixed mechanical problems, had parts flown in, got tired of rice and beans and coleslaw, and bounced off the occasional bottom in these shallow waters. But we also enjoyed swimming in clear, warm water, having wonderful sailing experiences, meeting interesting people, and making footprints on beautiful, untrod beaches. And, Shirley and I were a team. We learned to rely on each other and I gained an immense appreciation for her abilities.

After sailing nearly all of the Exuma and Abaco Islands, our return date loomed. We sailed back to Florida and up the inland waterway with many other "snowbirds" returning north for the summer. Here are some of our experiences in The Bahamas.

Royale Island Emergency

A horn honking woke us up. It was 2 a.m. We were at anchor at Royale Island, Abacos. I went up and saw that the large motor yacht that came in earlier had drug anchor and was just 20 feet in front of us. Its cockpit lights were on, engines were running, and the owner looked frantic. The wind was blowing and he was still dragging. A second sailboat appeared to be dragging anchor as well. My hunch was that the power boat had fouled the anchor chain to the other sailboat and probably ours, too.

I quickly donned my snorkel gear and swam over to the motor yacht. I yelled at the owner NOT to put the engines in gear and that I would attempt to untangle the anchors. He was very stressed, but seemed to understand. I found that his anchor had fouled the other sailboat's anchor chain and his anchor was dangling above the bottom, suspended by the sailboat's chain that he'd fouled. Thus, both the sailboat and motor yacht were pulling on the single anchor, and if not sorted out, the motor yacht would soon be upon us.

The water was cold and it was dark, but the lights from the motor yacht lit the water enough for me to see. After much effort and surfacing for gulps of air, I finally got the anchor chains untangled. I then boarded the motor yacht and told the owner to take up his anchor and move to the open area ahead and re-anchor with enough scope (more chain out) to hold the boat in the wind. I then swam back to our boat where Shirley had towels and hot chocolate, and helped me warm up. I was proud of what I was able to do and that next day, the owner of the motor yacht brought us a bottle of rum as a thank you.

Generator Blues

The generator suddenly quit with a "bang," belching acrid, burnt electrical smells. The small diesel motor was okay, but the electrical generator it ran was fried. We'd only been in the Bahamas for two weeks and our plans had to change. We needed the generator to run our water-maker to fill our water tanks, charge the batteries when the main engine is not running, use the microwave, and run the air compressor for filling the scuba tanks. None of this was essential, apart from having fresh water, which was only available in some areas, and it was expensive and of dubious quality.

After several high seas shortwave phone calls, I had a new generator unit shipped to Marsh Harbor. The plan was for me to meet it at the airport to clear it through customs and pay the duty. I rode my folding bike to and from the airport three times, with no sign of the generator. Waiting near the tarmac the fourth time, I saw what looked liked a crate that would hold the generator to load it onto the luggage cart. The cart was rolled to the open gate, then left. No one was around. I checked the label. Yes, this was it!

All the frustrations of changing plans, broken equipment, and disappointing rides to the airport erupted. While no one was around, I quickly grabbed the 50-pound box, got on my bike, and peddled off to the boat!! I later realized that I could have found myself in a Bahamian jail for cheating customs. This guilt was soothed once I spent the next six hours replacing the blown generator unit with the new—and it worked! Guilt turned into the kind of pride that only a tired, greasy man can know. Plus, we could now carry on with our sailing adventures.

Our unplanned stay at Marsh Harbor did have some highlights. We met two couples from two other cruising sailboats docked there and enjoyed their company for cocktail hour, dinner, and going about. We later sailed in flotilla to various places. One cool experience was attending Junkanoo—a traditional Bahamian celebration on New Year's Eve that starts at midnight with a wonderful parade featuring traditional music, dancing, and amazing costumes. It concludes several hours later with serving a local fish stew.

Rum Cay Excitement

The peaceful silence was abruptly broken. We had just gone below for our dinner after a beautiful sunset. It was interrupted by a deep rumble that vibrated through the boat. We jumped up to see what was happening. It was so dark, we could not make out the source of the throbbing rumble—until suddenly the beam of a huge searchlight from a very big US Coast Guard ship illuminated a large anchored motor yacht just 50 feet in front of it. The CG called the motor yacht on the VHF radio several times.

Finally, the call was answered by the owner who was ashore (on a portable, hand-held radio). The CG asked permission to board. The owner belligerently told the CG no way in a colorful way. After a heated exchange, the captain of the boat took the radio from the owner and wisely agreed that they would return to their boat and that the CG would indeed be able to board. Ultimately, the CG spent many hours aboard, probably inspecting every part of the boat. While this was going on, we noticed a CG launch passing by the stern of each boat at anchor, including ours, making notes of boat names and hailing ports.

We think this was about drugs! Earlier that day, we saw a twin engine plane circle over our anchorage a couple of times, then fly off. Then this large motor yacht came in and anchored. We think the drug authorities tracked the plane and thought a bundle of drugs (i.e. marijuana) may have been dropped for a motor yacht like this one that had just arrived to retrieve. We don't know if anything was found as we departed the next day.

Our days in the Bahamas were at a time when they were considered the drug highway from South and Central America to the US. We often saw low-flying helicopters with their side door open, exposing what would be a machine gun in Viet Nam, but was a camera photographing boats. A series of photographs over time would suggest to authorities any suspicious vessel movements.

In all our days of sailing the Bahamas, the Rum Cay event was the closest we came to a possible drug situation, *except* for a strange occurrence while at anchor up the mouth of a small river on Long Island. After a long sailing day, the only sheltered anchorage appeared to be up this river, which we navigated during low tide, bouncing off the bottom until well past the mouth. We saw no habitation or vessels anywhere. It was just getting light after a calm night. We were still in our bunk when we heard the motor of a small boat passing by. Looking out the aft ports, we saw a large, black inflatable with six men in dark wetsuits motoring up the river. It seemed so out of place. They did not bother us, but this did engage our imaginations about what they could be doing.

"Weathered in" at Staniel Cay

During the winter in the Bahamas, storms regularly passed through. The winds gained strength and clocked around in direction, making it difficult to find a protected anchorage. As one particular cold front approached, we took one of a handful of berths at the small marina on Staniel Cay.

When the wind blows 30 to 40 knots for days, it can get boring sitting in one spot, unable to enjoy calm water, beach time, or sailing. We met a couple on a large 55-foot sport fishing boat who invited us aboard to play bridge with them. It was an enjoyable diversion. They were an interesting couple. She was a granddaughter of Henry Flagler, who built the railroad on the east coast and "The Breakers" resort in Florida. She was describing her grandparents' boat to her husband by telling him it was the boat that had a boat similar to his, this 55-foot sport fisher, as the launch on its deck!

The Boaters' Social Scene

Elizabeth Harbor in the Exumas was about as far South as we got, and that's true for so many other boaters—even those who planned to go further South to the Caribbean. That's why it's called "chicken harbor," since many "chicken out" of going further, waiting for that perfect weather situation to go south that never seems to come.

But, the consolation (or result) is a vibrant social scene where one can join bridge games, beach volleyball, bingo, dinghy racing, beach barbecues, and more. It's all coordinated via the local VHF radio channel with morning updates on local boater news, weather, items for sale, and social events of the day. The result is that many boaters, either by choice or default, stay for the season or more.

Returning to the "Real World"

While we had planned to "sail away" for two years until our last-minute change of plans with Continental, it turned out better than *our* plan (as often happens). Sailing together on our own for six months was wonderful, but to do it for our planned two years would have turned a good thing into a lot less. We felt fulfilled by having new adventures, visiting new places, and enjoying the wonderful process of sailing. But this experience included the tedious aspect of dealing with variable weather, finding fresh provisions, coping with communications challenges (before cell and satellite phones), finding boat parts, and fixing things.

And although it was interesting to meet other cruisers from so many different places and walks of life, we had little to talk about aside from the weather, the best locations for the anchorages, where to buy fresh veggies, etcetera. Little news and few interests existed beyond life on the water.

After sailing through the night, heading for Stuart Inlet, Florida, a Coast Guard boat approached and called on the VHF radio. They wanted to board us! We were only about two miles from the harbor entrance.

"We're headed for the marina there," I told them. "Will you please board us once we get secure in a slip there?"

They agreed. Once tied up at the dock, four Coast Guard fellows clomped aboard and proceeded to remove, dislodge, and poke into and around every part of our dear boat. Of course, they found nothing of interest. But, this experience underscored the resources devoted to combating drug traffic. We were lucky, having heard stories of vessels' bulkheads, soles (floors), and interior paneling being broken apart in these searches. Hopefully they had good reason to suspect contraband in such cases.

From Stewart, we headed north via the intercoastal waterway, which goes all the way to New Jersey. As we motored along (very little sailing on this narrow passage) we passed small towns, lovely homes, wide estuaries, secluded bays, and miles of woods and swamps. The flip side were the many bridges that would either open upon request by radio or on a set schedule, requiring you to be there at the right time. Then we had to cope with the big power boats that spawned huge wakes in the narrow channels that would cause us to rock severely as they passed. Everything had to be well secured below.

After securing the boat at Coinjock Marina in North Carolina, we rented a car and drove to Boston to establish our ßnew home and resume a working life ashore. Several months later, I recruited two fellows to sail *Liberty* to her new home in Boston Harbor.

Important Lessons

- You can't really know even someone close until you have to rely on them for your safety and wellbeing. I learned how strong and able Shirley really is.
- A plan is simply a direction. Don't be so fixed on it that you miss opportunities to make it even better, even if it means changing it.

- It is amazing what we are capable of when called upon; like fixing things that appear baffling, doing what's needed even when seasick, helping others when you don't have to, responding to emergencies calmly and effectively.
- It takes immense planning, preparation, and disciplined effort to achieve what can be the most fulfilling experiences in life. But it is worth it!

Chapter 18

City Living—Life in Boston

A Big Adjustment

Living in a city was completely new to us. It took time to adjust to the constant activity, the din of background noise, and so many people everywhere! But the convenience of shops, restaurants, and groceries a short walk away, as well as the excitement and diversity of people and things to do, more than made up for the negatives.

Our first home was a small apartment on the waterfront, just 300 feet from my office. Great commute! We then moved to Marblehead, where we rented a house in the outskirts. It was pleasant, but the downside was the awful commute to work. We had been searching around Boston for an appealing location to buy a house. We discovered several nice communities, but they all required the lost time of commuting to work.

So, we focused on back bay Boston and bought a top-floor condo in a brownstone on historic Marlborough Street. It had been recently remodeled, but was small and the exterior and roof had never been properly restored. The elevator to our fifth floor was so small that two people had to be very friendly to fit! And, moving in required hiring a crane to lift our furniture up to and through the street side windows that had to be removed. City living entailed lots of new experiences!! But, the best part was the ability to walk to work.

This apartment had so many issues, we considered moving. A friend found an unfinished condo in a nearby brownstone that was being completely rebuilt. It was the top floor unit in a double-wide brownstone. A level 3,000 square feet, it had two decks, alley parking, and a big elevator. We hired a contractor to finish this end-unit that featured windows on three sides. The result was truly wonderful. When completed, we used "high end" decorators who had us leave for a weekend so they could "stage" all our furnishings and décor. Upon our return, we made our grand entrance to our new condo with *oohs* and *aahhs* and champagne. That's when we knew, "We had made it!!"

So, life was easy in the city. Everything was walking distance, including my office. The four-mile, round-trip walk to the office through the Public Garden, Boston Commons, and Faneuil Hall was beautiful and invigorating. We had an easy walk to the beautiful Christian Science Mother Church, which we attended regularly. Getting around was so easy that we went more than a year without a car. Driving around Boston is very challenging and, besides, our car, parked behind our building, was stolen—twice! We walked or took the subway, known as the "T." Whenever we went any distance, we rented a car. The airport was a cab ride away.

Our boat was berthed at the old Navy Yard in Charlestown near where the *USS Constitution* is berthed. That's the oldest Naval warship in commission. It fought in our Revolutionary War. Very little of it is original, but a tour will highlight those areas that are, especially in the keel section. It's a wonderful sight under sail—a living piece of our country's history that will give you goosebumps when seen under full sail.

We enjoyed sailing out of Boston Harbor and to Provincetown or points south. For our summer vacation, we loved sailing to Maine. It was an overnight sail. We still have very fond memories of quiet, foggy mornings in secure anchorages, taking the dinghy to a rocky shore and collecting buckets of large mussels, hiking on rocky islands picking blueberries, and hailing lobstermen from our dinghy to buy live lobster freshly caught at a bargain price.

A not-so-pleasant memory was hearing on VHF radio as we approached land after an overnight sail from Boston, that a hurricane was likely to reach the area within a day or so. To prepare, we found an empty anchorage with protection from the expected wind direction. We avoided the nearby harbor, which contained many moorings and anchored boats, since the biggest cause of damage in a hurricane is from boats dragging anchor or colliding with others. It took most of the day to deploy three anchors (one was 100-plus pounds), and take down the sails, awning, and dodger.

It was difficult to leave our precious boat, but we would be unable to do anything if we remained aboard in 80- to 100-plus knot winds. And it would be dangerous. We walked to that nearby busy harbor, where we stayed the night in the local yacht club, listening to weather reports and commiserating with others. As it turned out, the hurricane lessened in strength to a tropical storm after battering the coast south of Boston. Winds were very strong that night, but nothing like we feared. What a joy to walk back and spot our boat happily bobbing about and completely intact. We gratefully reassembled her and had a wonderful cruise.

Working at Headquarters

As wonderful as living in Boston was, my job wasn't. As executive vice president, I was responsible for half of the cable systems in the company, as well as the Marketing Department and Programming Departments in Boston. Four regional vice presidents reported to me. I found that I really missed regular interaction with front-line managers and employees. It is where I fit best, instead of dealing with high-level policy and financial matters and deal-making. Nevertheless, I cherished the company's values and ethics and had great respect for the key people I worked with.

My four operating regions included California. The Los Angeles area systems were a major challenge, as they faced major new-build construction to complete in some challenging conditions. Our operations included Compton and South Central—challenging places just to live, let alone build and operate cable systems. The riot resulting from the Rodney King trial was a major challenge, as it occurred in the midst of our operations.

Perry Parks, a football player who was black and had played football for the Rams, was the region manager who shared with me that while major damage and looting were occurring across the street from our South Central office, he had employees washing trucks in the open lot to signal that it was business as usual for us (although no trucks rolled that day) and we were there to stay. We experienced no damage.

The Compton mayor and staff were broadcasting from our local cable studio in Compton. They were giving updates and advice to viewers regarding the ongoing riots. They had lots of police protection. Soon the city manager told our office manager that they were leaving, along with their protection, and that we had better get our premises protected or suffer certain damage. Well, by then, every security service was committed and unavailable.

"Should we hire the only available company?" the manager asked.

"Who is it?" I asked.

"By Land, Sea or Air," the manager said.

References were unavailable, even if we'd had time to check them. They were well-armed and had monster camouflage painted trucks. The choices were both bad—chance it and suffer major damage, or hire "mercenaries" who might create some major legal challenges for us. I agreed to the mercenaries, so long as they made a show of their presence as a deterrence and hoped they would not have to do more than be visible. Fortunately, we suffered no damage and our "protection" did not have to go on offense.

Because we operated in a very decentralized manner, the only time I would get engaged in cable system operations was during annual budget review, when Region VP's had to defend their operating and capital budgets. What I loved about being a Region VP in Michigan was so long as I met or beat the agreed budgets, little interaction was required with Boston. And, I was given every resource to achieve good results.

The flip side was that being at headquarters in Boston, it was not consistent with this philosophy to engage with field operations unless asked for help. I did make many trips to local offices to meet with managers and employees to get a sense for how things were really going, apart from the numbers and to share the bigger picture of company values, priorities, progress, challenges, and successes. It was also an opportunity to listen to those working on the front line of their challenges, ideas, gripes, and suggestions. This continued to be the most rewarding part of my job.

A Second Try At Retirement

I had believed for many years that a job was for needed supply—to pay for what we need. Fulfillment came from within: from our sense of wellbeing, relationships, and passions. It's wonderful if that comes from a job, but it does not have to. I think I learned much of this when Shirley and I had to resolve the challenges brought by my choosing to quit that cable job in Portland to find "fulfillment" by owning and running those small businesses in Santa Cruz. But, my goal had never been to get rich or achieve status through business success. I've always thought that a job was a means to being able to "smell the roses"—to follow one's passions, to live a full life.

So, Shirley and I had another plan. I had been executive vice president for about three years. We figured five years would be enough, and by then, we would have the financial ability to really retire and go sailing again. This time, it would happen from a land base. So, on a trip to Sarasota, Florida to visit friends, Shirley found the perfect condo. It was located next to the performing arts center, an upscale shopping area, and the water, which provided a boat slip for our sailboat. Though I had not seen it, she bought it and announced it as my birthday present in early February!

Soon after, I was invited to lunch with our Chairman Amos Hostetter, and President Tim Neher. They offered me the position of president and chief operating officer of the company!! I was absolutely astounded, honored, and humbled. The idea of being president of this company—the most respected in the industry, the third largest with 8,000-plus employees—was an overwhelming honor. BUT, it meant changing our retirement plan and signing on to several more years at a challenging position. I told them I was planning to retire in two years or less and that I needed a month to think about this incredible offer. They were kind enough to allow this. So, we thought through all the implications of this incredible offer and decided to take the job. The next thing we did was sell the condo in Florida. We had stayed there two nights!! But, the dream of sailing off had not died.

Being president meant even higher-level challenges. I spent time in New York City, meeting with investment bankers who issued the bonds we sold to meet our capital requirements. I also met with bond-rating agencies who assigned the all-important rating on our bonds. I was more involved with negotiating our investments in programming services, programming carriage agreements, and speaking at industry conventions and conferences. This was in addition to overseeing the eight operating regions of the company.

I was also elected to Continental's board of directors. I gave operations reports at its quarterly board meetings and answered questions from these very insightful people. It was all a bit intimidating and I often felt ill-prepared to do the best at what was needed done. The people I dealt with and who reported to me were all very smart. Most were Harvard MBAs. Remember my dicey background and formal education at San Jose State College and night law school?!

Chapter 19

How and Why Did I Get Here?

A Balanced Life

I have often wondered what it was that helped me get to the lofty position I achieved, especially since it had not been my goal to get there. It wasn't an elite education, a killer résumé of experience, a network of influential mentors, or superior intellect. Sounding immodest, I think it was the quality of thought, values, work ethic, sincerity, and my apolitical nature that made a difference.

Achieving good results certainly helped, along with being in the right place at the right time. Paradoxically, I have a hunch that neither caring greatly about, nor seeking status, wealth and influence, it came to me anyway! These perks resulted from these qualities that I implemented.

"Your goal should be doing your best and having a balanced life," I had told my MSU students. "Success is a byproduct of this, and life will be much more fulfilling, even if the status and wealth does not follow. It is a win-win."

I did get some insight into my own "success" when a friend shared the following story with me. He was talking with an acquaintance who had just completed a survey of our company's employees to learn how they felt about the company, its practices, how they were treated, where improvements could be made, and more. This person said to my friend, "You know Mike Ritter. Why is it that he is so beloved in his company?" Wow, that really surprised and humbled me, but it gave me a subjective, partial insight as to why I got where I did, especially when "beloved" equates to "respected." Respect for a leader is essential to his or her effectiveness, and it must be earned and credible.

Thoughts on Wealth, Equality, and Children

From losing everything through our Santa Cruz fiasco, to becoming relatively wealthy, I've experienced both extremes. Yes, having wealth is better, but it does not insure happiness. I remember the days of our early marriage when we put cash in envelopes each month labelled Groceries, Gas, Rent, Entertainment, and so on. If the envelopes were emptied before the end of the month, we went without. Credit cards were rare. Back then, cards were just specific to gasoline companies or department stores. We paid cash or did without until we saved enough for the purchase. This applied to furniture, clothes, appliances, and cars. Our only debt was our mortgage on our duplexes. These were happy times. We knew where we stood and what we could afford, so we worked within that.

Since then, things have changed greatly, with a plethora of credit available to virtually everyone. At the same time, people are facing astronomical interest costs. Student debt is skyrocketing, thus limiting life choices for college graduates, and leaving nearly zero savings for many. An alarming statistic is that 40 percent of Americans cannot pay a $500 emergency bill, such as a car repair or an appliance failure. We badly need to educate young people about managing personal finances.

Having wealth has its own issues, even if not as stressful as those faced by the poorest among us. One is equality. Although I was the one who earned the salary and received the stock grants, I did not do it alone. Shirley largely raised our daughters, made a home of the many places we moved to when employment required, provided the emotional support we all needed, and performed countless daily chores. The value of her contribution to "my" success cannot be overstated.

We needed to demonstrate this understanding to our daughters. By the time they were in high school, they knew we were beginning to acquire some wealth. We decided to take them with us for an appointment with a lawyer to draw up an agreement between Shirley and me, setting forth that half of all our financial resources—including any more that we would acquire—would legally be half Shirley's and half mine. Although this is the law in community property states like California, it is not so clear elsewhere. This agreement demonstrated to Michelle and Lisa that their contributions to a marriage were absolutely equal to that of their future husbands, even if they did not work outside the home.

Another challenge facing those with wealth and children is how to handle gifting and otherwise provide for them without diminishing their incentive to work and be financially responsible. When do we tell kids we have wealth and how much do we tell them? Do we give them money outright, or set it aside for their specific future needs? How do we teach them about the value of hard work, financial responsibility, being charitable, and helping others? No single right answer exists for these questions. I think the most important instruction for them is the example we set for spending sensibly, avoiding credit, being philanthropic, and volunteering. We did our best, and gratefully, with good results.

The Third Time Is A Charm!

I had been president for several years when it became time to follow that dream we had put in abeyance. An heir apparent who could do the job extremely well reported to me. And we were in discussions with potential suitors to sell the company, which was at a crossroads. The cable TV business is very capital-intensive. Apart from the extensive cable infrastructure in the hundreds of communities we served, a pressing need existed to massively upgrade it to fiber optics and replace every customer's set-top converter boxes to those with advanced digital, high-definition, and impulse-ordering capability. The internet was beginning to explode, requiring the replacement of headend and cable-mounted electronics, and customer modems.

All this required huge capital investments. As a private company, the only way to do this was through even more debt, which was not feasible, given the leverage we already had. So, the choices were: go public or sell the company.

Going public via an IPO meant subordinating our priorities to those of Wall Street. Short-term, quarterly results drive stock valuations and analysis. Our long-term, high-quality service approach would be compromised. Life would not be as fulfilling or enjoyable. The alternative was to sell to a compatible buyer. This would secure a much higher price for the company than the IPO valuation would. This resulted in a number of suitors, discussions, and negotiations.

The successful buyer was Media One, the old Mountain States Telephone Company headquartered in Denver. The Continental purchase would be their foray into broadband. The price was good and the agreement was for cable operations headquarters to remain in Boston. This would allow many of our key people to remain with the new organization. It did not work out! Soon after acquisition, Media One demanded that headquarters be moved to Denver. This and other betrayals soured the aftermath of the deal. A lesson here was that no matter how good the financial package, it cannot erase the pain that a breach of promise and principle can bring.

Meanwhile, we had ordered a new sailboat that would be built in England. It was scheduled for delivery in May of 1995. While negotiations with Media One were progressing, our boat approached its delivery date. So, after 16 wonderful years with Continental, I retired to a very new adventure. We sold our dream condo in Back Bay and moved to our home at Lake Tahoe. Taking delivery of our boat, we hired a young English captain and began a sailing adventure that would eventually take us more that 50,000 miles, as far east as Turkey and west to Australia, over the next 10 years. Our boat was aptly named *Boundless*. Life's adventures continue!

"Boundless" racing across the Atlantic.

Afterword

WRITING THIS BOOK WAS a gift to myself. As I explored my memory, uncovering the significant details of my life, whether painful or pleasant, a growing sense of gratitude filled me as I saw and understood the goodness of all the connections that lifted my life. This strengthened my reliance on the Divine.

My goal in writing was to provide my family with my story, as it is partly theirs, and to share a few life lessons I learned along the way. I am no writer, as any reader would quickly note. So, I thought a simple, spiral-bound account would be sufficient. But, my wonderful advisors and publishers, Catherine Atkins Greenspan and her sister, Elizabeth Atkins, encouraged me to publish my book. Their more objective view of my story suggested that a wider distribution might help others see how their lives have been lifted by people and events of their past. The gratitude, confidence, and trust that comes from that insight is a powerful blessing.

The book ends with my retirement to begin my sailing adventure. What followed could easily be a separate book describing a 50,000-mile sailing odyssey. I sailed through most of the Mediterranean countries, Scandinavia, the U.K., Caribbean, New England, the Panama Canal, the South Pacific, New Zealand, and Australia. My wife, family, and several friends shared much of this adventure with me. A highlight was having our then nine-month-old grandson and his parents join us in the Galapagos Islands to remain aboard for another nine months, sailing more than 7,000 miles, and getting off in New Zealand when he was 18 months old!

Although I sold our magic carpet — *Boundless* — a few years ago, I continue to feed my sailing passion with a much smaller boat on San Francisco Bay, where I often single hand for several days. It is my meditation! Otherwise, my time is filled on the small farm we built near San Luis Obispo, CA, serving on several non-profit boards, being active in our church, doing some angel investing, and spending time with our four grandchildren who live within a 10 minute drive!

I continue to be "lifted."

Biography: Mike Ritter

SIMPLY SURVIVING A CHALLENGING childhood would be enough for most. Faced with family dysfunction, a variety of men cycling through, a step father's suicide, gangs, truancy, and a life threatening motorcycle accident, Mike did more than survive. A series of epiphanies gradually lifted him from laborer, to college student, law school graduate, lawyer and successful business executive. He ultimately became President and Chief Operating Officer of what was then the third-largest cable television company in the US.

Early in their marriage, Mike's wife, Shirley, decided they should take sailing lessons. This ignited a passion for sailing that led to Mike's early retirement and the ultimate dream of sailing over 50,000 miles around most of the world. He has since settled down with his wife and extended family on a small, organic farm near San Luis Obispo, California. Still a passionate sailor, he sails regularly on San Francisco Bay, and enjoys snowboarding when the snow flies in the Sierras.

Mike serves on several non-profit boards, is active in his church, and does some angel investing. Through his book, he hopes to share some life lessons and encourage others to look back with gratitude to see what and who have played a part in lifting their lives.

www.ingramcontent.com/pod-product-compliance
Lightning Source LLC
Chambersburg PA
CBHW020138130526
44591CB00030B/131